PREPPER
SURVIVAL GUIDE

KENNETH MCWILDE

TRAVEL NOTES

TABLE OF CONTENTS

BOOK 1
URBAN SURVIVAL

INTRODUCTION

You're quarantined in your home somewhere in the world, feeling that eerie mix of calm and panic. It's a concoction that makes your throat dry and your chest feel like it's about to explode. Or are those just symptoms of something more sinister?

The grocery stores have been all but emptied. Your favorite bar was boarded up after some hooligans raided it two nights prior. There's a church ten blocks away still serving chicken stew in Styrofoam bowls, but the police are standing by, keeping people from trampling one another. The police are enforcing curfew now too. No one's allowed out of their homes unless it's on the way to the hospital... or the morgue. Things are bleak. Too bleak.

You're wondering if now is the time to start preparing for the end. You've got a few cans of expired ham and beans, some rotten-looking potatoes, and a purple onion that has lived in this apartment longer than you have. Well, people have survived on less, right?

What if you could rewind to the time just before people were panic-buying in your city? To the time when the news showed more than just the death toll. You might have found this book right on time. After all, it is never too late or too complicated, or too crazy to prepare. Preparation takes no more strength than going grocery shopping. Preparation takes no more time than it takes to fill a backpack. Preparation takes no more knowledge than it takes to flip a page.

In what follows, you will find a comprehensive guide to stocking your shelves, gathering your team, and steeling your mind. For you will find that preparation is all about mentality.

Preparation Mentality

Panic is a sickness. It kills more people than a virus or a fire or a flood ever could. Panic makes us think that guns are more important than food. It makes us trample over other people just to get to what we need. Panic makes us stupid. Stupidity is deadly.

How do we avoid panic? The only cure for panic is preparation. Preparation is about being positive that you will have not only the necessities for survival, but also the purpose to move forward, the reason to keep pushing, keep adapting, keep thriving. Preparation ensures that your focus is always on how to make the most out of a bad situation, rather than facing that situation without any plan at all.

It is not outlandish, or conspiracy theorist, or overly zealous to prepare for a natural or manmade disaster. It is a basic facet of human evolution. We run scenarios through our mind, readying our body for the task at hand. The greatest test of our lives comes from the need to survive and if you are reading this then you understand your part to play in any extreme emergency.

It's not about trying to collect everything you can in a wild fear of what the future might bring. More than that though, it's about equipping yourself so that you can better serve your family, your friends, and your community.

Our Responsibilities

The urban environment is decidedly different from the wild, whether marine or mountainous, and it too presents dangers, albeit of a different kind.

We talk about overcrowding, pollution, crime, the presence of many buildings whose collapse is dangerous.

Dealing with a disaster in such a context requires the use of measures and the acquisition of knowledge and techniques quite different from those to be adopted in an outdoor environment.

Without neglecting the treatment of long-term preparation, we will preliminarily focus our attention on the moment of the BOOM, that is, the exact instant in which the disaster occurs and the moments immediately following, in the first 9 chapters the book will analyze the psychological status due to the trauma and will provide the technical knowledge necessary to save your life.

In the second phase, we will talk about the fundamental aspect that is the long-term preparation, aware that it must be organized in advance, in order to face the period of crisis that follows the "storm", arranging shelter, food and medicine supplies, etc.

Having planned a strategy that allows you to be prepared for even the worst, such as having to leave your home to move elsewhere, perhaps away from the built-up area, perhaps outdoors.

URBAN SURVIVAL prepares us for just that through the acquisition of survival skills, tactics and techniques that allow us to know how to operate in a densely populated urban setting should disaster strike.

SITUATIONAL AWARENESS

CHAPTER 1

Disaster preparation is, first and foremost, about awareness. Planning is a critical step in the process, but you also need to be prepared for the worst.

What are your specific needs? Where are vulnerable areas in your home or business? What would happen if there was no power for three days? How much water do you need to have on hand in case of emergency?

It's time to be proactive and think ahead. This will walk you through some simple steps that could make an all-too-real catastrophe less devastating.

Do You Have a Plan?

Making a plan will help you think realistically about handling a crisis and reducing the chance that panic will set in.

Create a Family Emergency Plan. Everyone needs to know their specific roles, including where they need to go, who they are going with, how they will get there, phone numbers for everyone involved, and how much food/water/clothing they should take. It's also essential for kids to know not to open the door for anyone until an adult says it is OK.

Understand Your Surroundings. Consider sandbagging as a way to mitigate flooding.

Have an Emergency Kit Ready. You should have supplies ready to go at all times. Think about what items you are most likely to need in the event of an emergency. The following are suggested things to keep in the kit:

Water, at least one gallon per person, per day for at least three days. Plan to use bottled water if you can't boil it for any reason.

Non-perishable food, including canned food, dried food, or ready-to-eat packets. Also include snack foods and crackers that can be eaten without heating, such as beef jerky or protein bars.

Clothing and personal items -- extra shoes, warm clothes for everyone in your family (wool hats and gloves), additional medication, or essential documents.

Flashlights and batteries.

A First Aid Kit.

Any special needs items, such as a portable toilet or a device to help those with disabilities.

Many of us believe that disaster preparation is too expensive or will take up a lot of time, but the reality is quite the opposite. Some preparation might just take a few minutes and some assembly, while others might take a day or two to complete with all of your supplies in place. These preparations could save your life in an emergency!

Planning may help you both mentally and financially as you work to restore the normalcy in your life. With a few simple preparedness items tucked away in an easily accessible space, like a hall closet or under the kitchen sink, you can minimize the potential disruption as well as lessen any potential financial strain that may result from such an unfortunate event.

I'm sure most people can associate with the following scenario: Your power goes off, you come home from work, and your house is as chaotic as if a tornado had just passed through. While this could have been prevented if preparedness items were checked beforehand, it's easier to shelve all those supplies than to address the needs of a family in crisis.

There are many different factors to consider: length of loss of power/water and the number of people residing with you. It's important to understand that having survival items stored in one place does not make it "prepared" for an emergency. Each item you have must be stacked, appropriately stored, and accessed in a crisis.

It doesn't matter if you're living in a place prone to earthquakes or tornadoes; everyone should know their risk level and what they can do about it before disaster strikes.

Disasters are sudden, destructive events that cause injury or death. They are caused by natural events like floods and earthquakes and human-made events like terrorist attacks and natural gas explosions.

A disaster is something that destroys or damages a large area, especially an unexpected, large-scale calamity.

A disaster can come from many sources: natural, industrial, and even accidental. You never know when a disaster will strike, but it's always wise to be prepared for the worst. Suppose you're an educator or work with children of any age. In that case, you may recognize how difficult it is to keep children safe in the event of a natural or environmental disaster. This explores what you need to do now to make sure they'll be safe later on.

Thankfully, some people study these disasters and help to mitigate their impacts eventually. They do this by educating other people on risk reduction and understanding the probability of these events occurring to provide sufficient warning time and advice on how best to manage them when they happen.

Natural disasters are typically distinguished from other types of disasters by a high impact event that contributes to the magnitude of economic or human loss, such as the eruption of Krakatoa in 1883. The resulting tsunami killed 36,000 people and destroyed two-thirds of homes in the Sunda Strait region. Other examples include floods or earthquakes that strike without warning and extreme weather, including tornadoes, hurricanes, and blizzards.

It is to have a disaster plan for your family. The unfortunate truth is that disasters can strike at any time, and when they do, the best of us can easily be undone.

Home Disaster Preparation

The phrase "home disaster" can conjure up images of floods, fires, or other terrifying dramas. It's always hard to find the right balance between predicting every potential disaster scenario and practicing a more hands-off approach.

One of these precautions is installing and maintaining an emergency water supply,

Although there's a common belief that bottled water will last for years if stored correctly in the right conditions, this isn't strictly true. Unfortunately, stored water does expire. It may not matter much if you're using the water for drinking or other purposes that don't require sterilization -but it can matter plenty if you need your stored supply for something like filling up a fish tank or for flushing toilets.

The CDC has some information on stored water and how long it can last under good storage conditions. Wherever possible, store your water in cool and dark places, and avoid temperatures below freezing. The CDC recommends against storing water in your garage or shed since they're too warm and prone to temperature fluctuations.

You'll want to make sure that any bottled water you use is appropriately stored for long-term use as well. Water that's packaged in glass bottles can last indefinitely as long as it's kept sealed and out of direct sunlight or excessive heat. Biodigester says that plain old water stored in plastic bottles will last for at least a year. Still, if you're concerned about potential microbiological contamination, it's best to avoid keeping the water mixed with other liquids.

The CDC recommends using food-grade plastic storage bottles when storing your bottled water. That way, even if you have to keep the bottles in your car or basement, they can't get contaminated by airborne microbes, and you don't run the risk of them exploding due to temperature changes.

Another precaution is notifying family members and friends of your home's location and layout so that they can be on alert for intruders. The Red Cross recommends letting friends and relatives know where you store important things like emergency kits and first aid supplies, as well as where you keep an extra key for the house.

Water and Sewer Backup Prevention, Preparation, and Cleanup Tips

Water and sewer backup happens when service lines that bring water or sewage to your home are damaged.

In some cases, the service line may be completely severed. This can happen if a pipe suddenly bursts near the property line or if an object punctures or collapses the tube.

More often than not, service lines are just cracked by soil settling underneath them over time. The cracks can gradually turn into holes as more pipes are disturbed and become unhinged.

Once a crack forms, it is only a matter of time before the pipe collapses. To avoid this, inspect your property lines for signs of damage or sagging.

If there is evidence of damage, have the service lines checked immediately. The longer you wait to get them repaired, the greater the chances that they will fail and leak water into your home.

If you find cracks or holes in a sewer line, be sure to clear out the water and sewage that has been trapped inside. This will lower the chances of flooding in your home and make it easier for professionals to fix the pipes.

If water or sewage has already entered your home, try to clear the area of any standing water as swiftly as possible. This involves using towels, buckets, or mops to soak up as much water as you can. Be sure not to disturb any electrical equipment while doing so, especially near standing water.

Once this process is complete, you will want to do a more thorough cleaning with specialized equipment designed for disaster recovery. These types of tools are designed to remove any dirt or debris that may have been left behind.

Once you are done cleaning, you will want to dry out the area as much as possible. Plastic sheeting, towels, and other materials will help seal up any potential leaks before they have a chance to occur again.

First, you want to remove any standing water as soon as possible to reduce the chances of mold growth. Next, make sure the area is adequately ventilated. You can do this by opening windows and doors and using fans to create air flow.

After that, proceed with cleanup by removing all debris and damaged materials from the area. Throw away anything that cannot be salvaged and carefully clean any remaining items with a disinfectant spray or solution.

Remember to wear protective gear whenever handling potentially hazardous materials like wood or metal shards from broken belongings.

If a flood, earthquake, or other disaster disrupts your water and sewer services, you'll need to take precautions. Once the flood has passed, make sure to clean up any sewage backup that might have occurred in the area.

Let's start with what you should do before a disaster occurs. If there's an impending storm forecasted that may cause flooding or if there's been an earthquake nearby, it's best to prepare now so that when the storm hits, you're ready. FEMA has a list of what you should do before, during, and after an event that may cause flooding. The following are some of their recommendations.

Before a Storm

If you have time, move valuable belongings to upper floors or higher ground. If the water levels rise above your first floor, anything above it will be safe from damage. You can also place items in plastic containers to help keep them dry if they can float if need be.

Dry your wet basement or crawlspace with fans if a flood is expected.

Lock up your valuables, and move tools to higher levels if they are in lower areas such as basements or first floors. Keep a list of what was where and use it to repurchase items later.

Don't forget about your garage! Move vehicles to higher ground and remove all fuel sources that may leak during the flooding. FEMA recommends keeping one gallon per person on hand per day for at least three days during extreme weather situations.

If you have a basement or crawlspace, make sure it's dry (or at least higher than the expected flood level). If this isn't possible, fans should be placed in the area to help dry the space quickly.

Before an Earthquake

After an earthquake, there's likely going to be water damage throughout your home.

With any earthquake, beware of the possibility of aftershocks. Be sure to go to a safe location away from windows or walls that could break, and follow instructions calmly.

After an Earthquake

Don't forget that a significant earthquake can also result in water damage. Aftershocks can cause cracked walls and other structural damage if they occur after the fact. If you're not sure, ask your agent for more information before deciding what to do next. If you've damaged your home, contact a local contractor to help with repairs.

Don't forget about your garage! Keep it closed and locked until the water has been drained from it. If you lose power, water, or gas due to the earthquake, your garage doors could be in danger. Leave them open until strength is repaired and utility services are working again.

Safer Home in Case of a Tsunami or Earthquake

A tsunami is an ocean wave caused by the displacement of a large volume of water. Earthquakes or volcanoes can cause tsunamis, and many homes are not built to withstand these natural disasters. This will show you how to make your home safer in case of a tsunami or earthquake.

You may have seen how houses are destroyed in movies about natural disasters, but luckily for you, these tips will help keep your house safe from tsunamis and earthquakes. There are many simple ways to reinforce the stability of your home so that it is prepared for any natural disaster. Understandably, this can be a considerable expense for homeowners and renters alike, but it's a worthy investment if you want peace of mind.

1) If walls are weak, try to build them extra strong. Another tip for strengthening walls is to install steel studs. This will make the walls more vigorous and will reinforce them against earthquakes and other natural disasters. To add more reinforcements, you can also use steel beams that are bolted into the wall.

2) You will want to reinforce the roof. Depending on how high your house is, you might want to back it with some type of solid mesh or additional steel beams installed underneath your home for support.

3) If your house is reinforced against earthquakes, you may want to consider installing some flood defense systems. This can help protect your home from flooding if there is a nearby river or large body of water.

4) Ensure that you have enough clearance from walls for the water to flow through. To keep enough room, you might want to use a space between your walls and the roof or floors above them.

5) You might also want to consider installing a permanent sump pump in case of

flooding due to an earthquake.

6) Consider placing some heavy furniture on the lower levels of your home. This will help weigh the house down and will give it additional reinforcement. Try to stack heavy objects like bookshelves, televisions, and other large appliances on the lower levels of your home to add more weight to it.

7) Many homes will have walls that aren't reinforced against earthquakes or tsunamis, so installing some type of additional foam or rubber barriers will help minimize the damage done by these natural disasters. These fences can also keep out any harsh winds and rain when things are calm once again.

8) If you have some type of barbeque or smoker, try to move it. You don't want to have it topple over when the ground shakes. Move the smoker off of any deck or patio and place it in the garage. This is a precaution that can save you a lot of trouble if your house is shaking due to an earthquake or other natural disaster.

9) It's also essential to make sure that all electrical devices are protected as well. Move any electrical appliances, like televisions, out of cabinets.

10) Consider completely removing your walls and moving into a trailer.

11) If you live near a large body of water, it's also essential to take some precautions.

If we talk about safety, another important thing we should mention is taking care of yourself physically. It's essential to stay healthy and active. You can prevent many of the diseases that can occur with a poor diet. Try to reduce your sugar intake, and eat more fresh fruits and vegetables. Even if you have a healthy diet, you should still wear sun-protective clothing on hot days. And make sure your safety is secured when you are going outside.

Those are some of the essential tips to keep your home safe from earthquakes or tsunamis in case of an earthquake or tsunami.

WHAT IS A GET HOME BAG

CHAPTER 2

Do you ever get that feeling in your gut that there is something wrong? Pangs of anxiety, like a warning bell, ringing in your head as you feel the tension building. While I cannot say what it is specifically that makes this feeling so strong, I can assure you that many other people have felt this way before and it's nothing to worry about.

As a prepper and an urban survival expert, I want to make sure all readers are prepared for the worst scenario possible: the day where everything goes wrong. In case of any emergencies or disaster, it's important to always be prepared by having a Get Home Bag (GHB) on hand at home or work.

A Get Home Bag is a survival kit that's packed with essential items to help you in any urban or rural environment. It's also called a Bug Out Bag (BOB), but keep in mind that these two are not the same. While a BOB is just a larger version of a GHB, some people will use the term "Get Home Bag" to include both small and large GHBs. So, don't worry about getting confused between these two terms as we're only going to discuss small GHBs here.

A Get Home Bag is a kit that is designed to help you get back home quickly and safely in an emergency. There are many types of Get Home Bags depending on the situation. For example, if you are hiking, your pack will not require any water or food because it is not going anywhere. On the other hand, bags specifically designed for natural disasters and civil unrest are much more comprehensive.

What it Must Contain

The components of a Get Home Bag will vary, depending on your personal needs and the environment you live in. However, there are certain items that can be found in almost all GHBs. These include:

Water: At least 1-3 liters, depending on personal needs & environment.

Food: At least 1-3 days of nonperishable & lightweight food items.

First Aid Supplies: Bandages and disinfectants for minor injuries.

Sanitation Supplies: Toilet paper, kitty litter or other absorbent materials for waste management.

Gear: Clothing, flashlight, matches/lighter & pocket knife.

Cash: Small bills and change for phone calls and transportation in case of an emergency.

The Get Home Bag also allows one to carry any supplies you may need to take with you in the event you leave your home or office at a moment's notice. This can include whatever supplies your family may need if you are forced to evacuate your home quickly in the event of a natural disaster or civil emergency, such as extra clothing, shoes, important papers and medications such as insulin for diabetics. The Get Home Bag allows you the freedom to save other items for a more secure environment.

Differences Between GHB and BOB

There are many people who have a get home bag and a bug out bag. Other people only have one of these bags, but they don't understand the difference between them. We will explain what is in each type of bag, and how they are different.

A get home bag is smaller than a bug out bag, so it's easier to carry around in your car or in your backpack if you're traveling by foot. It has enough supplies for you to survive for 24 hours outside of the house, but it's not designed for more than that so it doesn't have items like spare clothing that could be destroyed by weather conditions during a long-term emergency situation.

Here are some of the differences between these two types of bags:

In a get home bag, your entire family doesn't need to carry it with them because it's small enough to be carried by one person if necessary. In a bug out bag, everyone needs to have their own bag, so you can't take your wife's bag and leave yours at home. In a get home bag, you could take the essentials and put anything else you don't need in the car or on a separate pack. In a bug out bag, you need to carry the bug out bag with all of your supplies so that it is easy to find what you need in case of an emergency at night when it's dark. If someone took your bug out bag with them, they would need to replace everything that was in your bug out bag if they lost it.

In a get home bag, most people can carry everything they need while they are on foot. Some people might need to use a bicycle or a kayak if they live in an area where it's too far for them to walk, but it's possible for anyone to be able to get home on foot by carrying their get home bag. In a bug out bag, your vehicle will probably be your only option for getting away from danger if you are completely stuck in an area that you can't get out of.

A get home bag is designed so you are still able to sleep comfortably outside of the house. In a bug out bag, you need to be ready to move and stay outside for quite some time because it will take you a long time to get back to the safety of your home.

You can have a get home bag for surviving with your family if something terrible happens. You might not have enough food or water, but it's still better than being completely cut off from the outside world. In a larger bug out situation, there is no guarantee that your area will be cut off from the rest of the world. You could have enough supplies in your bug out bag that you could survive for a long time if things go wrong with the communication system and electricity, but there's no guarantee that this will happen due to other reasons. A get home bag is good for a small area and will last you a day or two. A bug out bag is better for an entire region or even the country, because it will last you months.

In a bug out bag, you need to take care of each and every item. If you put your machete in your bag and it rips the machete bag or if the zipper gets stuck on the backpack when you are carrying it, then you can't get to it. You might not have anything to replace it with because all of your tools are in your bug out bag.

Get home bags are meant to get you back to the safety of your home, whether that's in a few hours or a few days. In an emergency situation, it's very unlikely that someone will come to help, and if they do come to help and there is already no electricity or heat running, then you are going to have trouble keeping all of these items cold enough. There is no guarantee that the electricity will be restored at any time during the emergency situation, so you could run out of food and water before help comes. Your family is not going to want to wait around in a cold house because they still need to go about their normal lives in case something bad happens with your ability to get away from danger.

A bug out bag is meant to take you away from danger. If you are leaving your home because of a hurricane, then there is no guarantee that the hurricane will go in a particular direction and hit your house alone. Hurricanes have the ability to wipe out entire cities, so it's important to have a bug out bag ready if you are worried about what could happen.

If something bad happens while you're on vacation, then your get home bag will be able to help at least until someone comes to help. In a bug out situation, if they don't come to help soon enough, then you won't survive long with all of these supplies in your bug out bag.

In a bug out situation, you need to be able to survive for an extended period of time (at least a month or two). A get home bag only needs to last you for a few days. In the case of a hurricane, it's entirely possible that the power and water will be restored in just two or three days, so all of your supplies in your bug out bag could be fine as long as they are still cold enough.

A get home bag is designed to help you make it through the first few days when something bad happens.

For the majority of people, they are going to want more supplies in their homes than just water and food. You will want to stock up on at least one gallon of water per person every day. You will probably also want to have at least two weeks worth of non-perishable food items stored in your bug out bag. You can find non-perishable foods that are easy for you to find when you go shopping for groceries, like canned meats and vegetables. You might want to use things that you normally eat at home so that you don't have to worry about finding different foods during an emergency situation.

If you live in an area where you might be able to get by without a bug out bag, then there are lots of supplies that you won't need in your get home bag. For example, if the only thing that goes wrong in the area is a tornado and the power goes out for about a day or two, then this is going to be enough time for your family members to have enough water and food stocked up in their homes. In this case, they will only need to keep this emergency kit in their car. They can fill this kit with the necessary supplies for a couple of days and then when the power comes back on, they can stock their home up again.

You need to be able to stock up on water and food so that your family is not going to have any problems when they go to get groceries.

URBAN EDC (EVERY DAY CARRYING)

CHAPTER 3

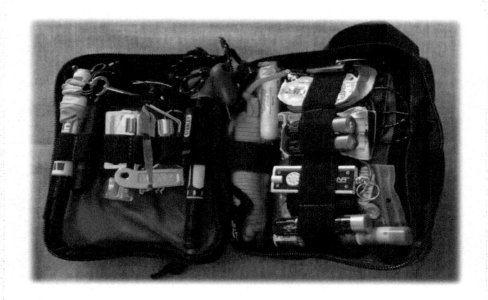

If you find yourself in a situation for which you don't have the GHB immediately at hand, how do you get to it? How do you get out of a critical situation, for example if you are trapped in an elevator, or an enclosed location? You would like to get out, free yourself but you don't have the GHB because it's in your car, or office and you need to get to it because you will need that, in turn to get to your home. You need an Urban EDC

The Urban EDC is an even more specific tool than the GHB. It is an ultra-compact survival kit that you can carry with you at all times, containing useful, readily available items and gadgets that can fit in a container of minimal size, easy to carry and Legal Friendly while also being economical.

To build an EDC you will need to consider:

- Must serve for all kinds of emergencies

- How much space do I have available, i.e., overall dimensions?

- How much does it need to weigh?

- Who will use the kit: Adult? Children?

- What type of item is not allowed to be carried by law?

- It should only contain tools that I can actually use.

Urban EDC (Every Day Carry) is all about the items that we keep with us on a regular basis.

It's an age-old tradition to have a kit or box of essential tools and supplies on hand at all times, ready to be deployed in an emergency or if your home was unoccupied for an extended period of time.

But modern society doesn't require the same level of preparedness as our ancestors' did. The equipment in Urban EDC kits is much more focused on enhancing our daily lives.

We've all seen the photos of the rugged, yet well-dressed, man holding an expensive looking watch in one hand and a $500 pen in another. They're images that can inspire you to study throwing knives or learn how to tie fancy knots.

But you don't have to be a survivalist or Rambo to carry a useful and interesting kit. Most city folk don't need as much gear as people in rural areas. But there are still plenty of items that can make your life easier and more fun.

What is EDC

EDC stands for "everyday carry" or "every day carry". It's a personal collection of items that people keep on their person, all the time. Basically, it's just like a pocket full of tools and tricks to make life easier.

The modern concept of EDC has been around since the late 90's. It's generally recognized as an extension of prepper culture in which people prepare for every day environment threats. The term "prepper" was originally used by the US military to describe someone who might be drafted at a moment's notice and sent abroad to fight with their country overseas. For example, the term was used to describe people who were ready to be drafted at a moment's notice in the event of World War II.

Today, "prepper" has come to refer more generally to a person who is always prepared for anything. Some simple preppers keep extra food and water on hand in case of natural disaster, while some others go further and set aside supplies like fuel and extra cash just in case some life-or-death situation comes up. The original concept of being ready for military draft is now mostly obsolete as military conscription has ended worldwide, but many believe that prepper culture still has value by teaching people how to be better prepared for any situation they might encounter in their daily lives.

EDC is a specific part of prepper culture that deals with daily life. It focuses on the most likely threats that might happen every day and prepares one to be able to deal with them. Usually, this means carrying some sort of tool like a knife or flashlight that can be used in a variety of small, everyday scenarios.

A simple example would be someone who always keeps a pocket knife with them so they can open boxes, cut twine on something, or cut their nails in case the need should arise. EDC is really just an extension of the Boy Scout's motto: "Be Prepared".

The idea of EDC is that if you're at the grocery store and some bad guy tries to mug you, a simple pocketknife can save the day. If you're hiking in the woods and only have a simple lock to secure your backpack, maybe a rock or stick will work as well.

As always with this sort of thing, an ounce of prevention is worth a pound of cure. Always be smart and prepared when it comes to dangerous situations and they won't happen in the first place. However, life is not always ideal and sometimes you might find yourself in an emergency situation.

Often, EDC items are chosen by the user based on their own personal preferences. One person might like a small multi-tool while another prefers something larger like a folding knife. One might carry a simple pen while another keeps a full-size flashlight as part of their EDC collection.

The basic idea behind EDC is that every day items should be simple, basic, and easily accessible. This will allow the user to operate more effectively wherever they are without having to pull out a bunch of extra things they don't really need.

Like other prepper concepts, it's commonly used as a way of building motivation and improving self-sufficiency. EDC is also a good way to introduce new people to the concept as a whole and educate them on what it means to be prepared for everyday life threats.

EDC: What it Must Contain

These are essential items that every person should carry at all times. EDCs may vary from person to person, but these are the most important aspects and must never be left out.

What items should go in your EDC?

-Carry a flashlight. Flashlights are essential not only because they are used to light up the dark, but also because they can be used for numerous other purposes like finding anything inside your bag or your car, or just plain ambushing an unsuspecting thief to do the dirty work for you. Definitely a must have item for your EDC.

-A knife (should be fixed and non-folding). This is also what most people come up with when asked of the things you should carry on your person. The uses of a knife are too many to list, but here a few: Self defense, opening boxes and packages, cutting cable ties, stripping wires and cables, etc.

-A lighter. The best use for a lighter is to start a fire in case you can't reach your matches or lighters when an emergency arises. You can also use it as an emergency light source by using any flammable materials that you can find around you (e.g. newspapers and books).

-A bottle of water. A bottle of water should be carried in your bag at all times. You can use them for numerous purposes ranging from protection from the elements, to hydrating yourself during a long hike, to washing yourself during an emergency, etc.

-A pocket knife (preferably a pocket knife that is fixed and non-folding). This is also an essential item in my personal EDC. It has many uses: opening boxes, stripping wires and cables, cutting cable ties (as mentioned before), cutting string and wire to make different things (i.e. traps, traps for small animals, etc), and of course, self defense.

-Car keys (along with other keys that you may have. These include door keys, your dorm/room's key and maybe even a locker key). Car keys are an obvious one for most people but not to others. It is pretty self explanatory though: if something happens that making you have to drive your car somewhere in an emergency but your car is locked inside a parking lot or garage, then obviously you need the car keys to get out.

-A multitool (preferably one that has pliers in it). Multitools can be used for many things and they can always help you out in a pinch. Its usefulness is self explanatory by just looking at it.

And that's it! The five items above are essential and should never be left out of your EDC kit. Some people may also choose to include more items into their EDC, but everything listed above are the most important items that everyone should carry with them at all times.

BASIC FIRST AID TECHNIQUES
URBAN FIRST AID KIT

CHAPTER 4

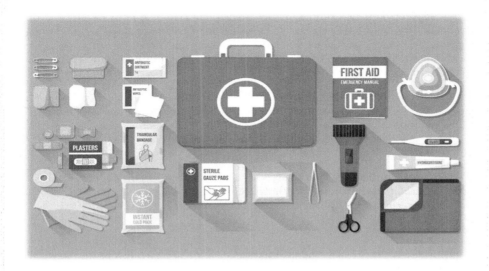

In the event of an emergency, it's best to be prepared. That way, you won't have to carry a heavy bag of essentials or spend valuable time digging through drawers and closets trying to find anything that could be used. Also keep in mind that if you are in the outdoors you will need items like a knife, sunscreen, bug spray, raincoat and waterproof matches for emergencies.

A good kit should include bandages and first-aid items for cuts and scrapes, tweezers for removing splinters (and ticks), a thermometer, pain relievers, antiseptic towelettes, and anything else you think you might need. Don't forget to pack extra medication that you take on a daily basis. It is also important to pack non-perishable food items in case you need sustenance quickly.

Make sure the kit is properly stored in an easy to carry container. If possible store it where you can grab and go in an emergency such as right by the front door or near the bedside table.

Survival First-Aid Kit

A well-stocked first-aid kit can be the difference between life and death. In a survival situation, an injured person may have to wait hours or days for help — and with a severe injury, you may not have any help at all. You want your first-aid kit to give you the best chance of successfully treating injuries and illnesses until professional medical help arrives.

With an adequate supply of medicines, bandages, and sterilizing tools, you can take care of yourself and help those around you when you don't have access to medical facilities. Don't go by what you see in first aid kits in local stores.

Sutures and Sterilizing Materials

For most emergencies, sutures are not needed, but they should be included if you have room in your kit. They are used to close cuts and lacerations, as well as for internal bleeding. For thread, use dental floss since it is strong and already waxed at the ends. Alcohol-based antiseptic can be used before stitching incisions together to disinfect the wound from bacteria and other germs.

Tape is suitable for holding sutures in place, but duct tape may be more practical, especially if you have a larger wound. For butterfly bandages, buy the Steri-Strips instead of the traditional kind as it seals wounds better and heals faster. If you have a Mylar blanket or any other metallic or reflective material, you can use it to reflect sunlight on the damage for faster healing time.

Antibiotic ointments, such as Neosporin, can be used to apply on wounds to prevent infection. Chlorhexidine antiseptic should also be included since its use will prevent disease and keep bacteria from spreading under the stitches or bandaging.

Infection Control

Antibacterial hand wipes should be used to disinfect hands before touching any wounds. You don't want to spread bacteria around and cause an infection, so avoid using public restrooms. You can also use sanitizer gel or spray on your hands before touching anything.

A total body cleansing station with lancets, alcohol swabs, alcohol wipes, a thermometer for checking body temperature, and a thermometer tape measure would be suitable for assisting in the primary care of wounds.

A portable foot bath can be used to clean wounds and disinfect foot ulcers. It is suitable for cleaning, but it does not have any antibacterial agent, so the damage will still get infected.

Any medical tape or bandages can be used as long as the FDA approves them. Please make sure they are latex-free and approved for use on human skin or wounds. You may also want to choose a specific brand of medical tape since some may contain silicone - a substance that may cause irritation or burning of your skin, especially when you don't notice it immediately.

Bandages, Splints, and Slings

An emergency kit is a must-have for a home or car. But don't forget to replenish your supplies every year!

A common misconception is that sterile gauze, bandages, slings, and splints are only used in emergencies. However, these everyday items should be included in an emergency kit. They can also be used as part of a daily routine in the medical field.

Bandages can limit swelling and stop bleeding by absorbing blood after an injury to the area where they are applied. Slings help immobilize an injured limb while taking pressure off the injured joint or spine nearby. Splints can help stabilize a broken limb or broken bone until it is healing or has been set.

Items to Include in an Emergency Kit

Include the following items:

Gauze, bandages, slings, surgical tape, antibiotic ointment, alcohol swabs, butterfly bandages, gauze pads, non-stick pads, or waterproof adhesive strips minor cuts and scrapes. Cotton swabs should be included as well for cleaning wounds after applying antibiotic ointment. 3x3 gauze dressings.

For home kits, including a large gauze pad to stop bleeding from significant wounds, such as those that result from deep cuts and punctures. These are best used with a splint to secure the gauze in place.

If you use band-aids for more than one day, you want to replace them with a new one each day.

Wrap the gauze around the affected area gently with the ointment underneath for protection against germs or bacteria. You can also apply non-stick pads after cleaning and removing debris from an injury to keep it clean and separate it from clothing or other items during transport.

Pet slings are for dogs and cats that get into mischief. To aid in their mobility or prevent pain while healing, they can be used with a small doggie bed or on top of your grandmother's wheelchair.

Antiseptic Wipes and Bandages

Emergencies often require quick action, and sometimes store-bought supplies just aren't cutting it. Fortunately, you have a lot of natural remedies at your disposal! Countless plants worldwide have been used traditionally to disinfect wounds, fight infection, and prevent illness. These are some of our favorites.

Antiseptic Wipes and Bandages for Emergencies

1. Jambu Air

Jambu air is a native tree from Indonesia used traditionally to heal wounds of all kinds. Its leaves contain antiseptic compounds (including eugenol!) with anti-inflammatory, astringent, antibacterial, and antifungal properties. You can apply these leaves directly onto wounds or crush them up to make an infusion to apply to the injury.

Visitors to the island will also tell you a story of how this tree saved the life of a child who a saltwater crocodile almost ate. The child could defend himself by hitting the crocodile with a branch, but the sting of the branch's poison left him badly poisoned. A Jambu air leaf was used for bathing the child's wounds, and he was able to recover.

2. Bark

The bark of the American sumac and related plants contains a natural compound (submachine) that provides antiseptic, antiviral, and anti-inflammatory properties. It's known to be good at preventing infection when applied directly to wounds (traditional Native American uses this treatment) but is also very effective when mixed with a bit of alcohol to make a wound dressing.

In a small pot, put 2-3 fresh or dried sumac branches in 1 cup (240 ml) of water.

Cover and allow to steep for 2-3 days, then strain. Add the strained liquid to a bandage or wound pack.

3. Roots

Most roots are full of antioxidants, and many have anti-inflammatory properties. Sources from the Queen's delight plant (Stillingia sylvatica) are traditionally used to improve circulation and heal wounds. Apply these directly to the injury.

4. Leaves and Berries

The leaves and berries of various plants, particularly the common mulberry tree, have antibacterial properties that make them helpful in treating skin infections. The leaves also contain salicylic acid, which makes them effective at fighting pain caused by an open wound!

Create an infusion:

In a small pot, steep 2-3 fresh or dried leaves in 1 cup (240 ml) of water for 1 hour. Strain and add to a bandage or wound pack.

5. Tea Tree Oil

Tea tree oil is known for its antibacterial and antifungal properties, making it a great addition to any first aid kit! It's beneficial for treating skin infections caused by bacteria and fungus, as well as ear infections.

6. Plantain Leaf

Plantain leaves are traditionally used in North America to treat insect bites, stings, and skin irritations like eczema. Fresh leaves are also used to treat common colds and can be used as a tea or made into an infusion that can be taken internally.

7. Aloe

Aloe vera is known for its anti-inflammatory properties, making it a great addition to any first aid kit! It's also helpful in helping wounds heal quickly, relieving pain, and treating skin irritations (including sunburns and other forms of burns). If using the aloe as a topical treatment, mix in some honey for extra soothing qualities.

8. Rice Bran Oil

Rice bran oil contains fatty acids that are known to have anti-inflammatory effects on the skin. It is also known to have a fungicidal effect, making it helpful in treating fungal infections on the skin or nails.

9. Cloves

Cloves are part of the myrtle family and are known for their antiseptic and analgesic properties. Clove oil can be mixed with toothpaste to relieve the pain of teething babies and applied directly onto wounds (or put into a bandage or wound pack).

10. Tea

Most teas are helpful as topical treatments for wounds.

Stress tea (white tea, green tea, chamomile) has anti-inflammatory and antimicrobial properties that make it great for encouraging wound healing and pain relief. It's also used to relieve pressure on the throat and for its calming effects.

Chamomile contains compounds known as flavonoids that have antioxidant properties that can help decrease tissue damage. Chamomile's anti-inflammatory properties also mean it can help treat skin irritations or burns.

11. Soap Nuts

Soap nuts are dried fruits from trees in the Sapindaceae family that contain saponins, which have antibacterial and antifungal properties. Soak 10-15 soap nuts overnight in 2 cups (480 ml) of water, then use the liquid to wash wounds daily.

12. Baking Soda

Baking soda (sodium bicarbonate) is an excellent topical disinfectant for wounds and other scrapes and abrasions. Swab it on multiple times per day to prevent infection. If the damage does get infected, or any bacteria manage to enter your body through your open wound, then you should see your doctor.

13. Aloe Vera

Aloe vera is an excellent topical treatment for burns, skin irritations, and wounds. You can drink aloe vera juice to promote digestion and increase energy levels or apply pure aloe vera gel directly to wounds for faster healing.

14. Plantain

This common weed is known for its anti-inflammatory and wound healing properties, mainly when applied in combination with echinacea root tincture. Plantain also helps relieve pain, blisters, swelling, and itching at the site of an injury or wound. To extract it, dig a large hole and place the plant in the center of it. Dig out the plant with your hands, and then rub the root against itself as much as possible. The plant is ready to eat when it splits open into three parts.

15. Honey

Applying honey to wounds is one of those old-fashioned remedies that work wonders in healing open wounds fast. For best results, use raw honey directly to the injury, or mix with another healing ointment like aloe vera gel for more optimal results.

16. Calendula

Calendula is a flower that can be turned into an infusion and taken internally to treat ulcers, gastritis, and hemorrhoids. You can also apply the infusion directly to wounds or make a salve of calendula and coconut oil to soothe skin irritations.

17. Chamomile

A chamomile compress helps treat inflammation of the skin, such as insect bites, stings, rashes, and skin irritations caused by trauma or allergic reaction.

18. Coconut oil

Coconut oil is an anti-fungal treatment for athlete's foot, ringworm, and jock itch. It is also effective on psoriasis, acne, warts, and various skin problems caused by dandruff. According to Ayurvedic culture, melts are placed in oiled areas of the body as a type of mosquito repellent when not being used in cooking.

Medical Emergency Survival Guide

Panic can be as dangerous to our health as the conditions that caused it.

With the recent increase in medical emergencies and the ever-increasing complexity of healthcare, it's never been more critical to have a plan.

Stay Calm: Panicking won't solve anything and will only make you weaker. Utilize your resources: Ask for help! Find somebody who can communicate with doctors or nurses and find out what you need to do. If no one is there, call an ambulance (or dial 911). Keep breathing as deeply as possible to maintain oxygen levels in your body.

Panicking won't solve anything and will only make you weaker. Utilize your resources: Ask for help! Find somebody who can communicate with doctors or nurses and find out what you need to do. If no one is there, call an ambulance (or dial 911). Keep breathing as deeply as possible to maintain oxygen levels in your body. Don't fight the needle: The ER doctor knows precisely what they're doing, but try not to resist the IV insertion if you have a vein. You can cause yourself too much trouble by fighting against it and perhaps accidentally breaking it.

The ER doctor knows precisely what they're doing, but try not to resist the IV insertion if you have a vein. You can cause yourself too much trouble by fighting against it and perhaps accidentally breaking it. Don't be shy: Ask the first person you see if they can help. If they're a patient, explain that your loved one was admitted to the ER with suspected heart failure and ask them to notify their doctor. If a nurse is working, tell them what's going on so they can call for help (if they're on-call).

Ask the first person you see if they can help. If they're a patient, explain that your loved one was admitted to the ER with suspected heart failure and ask them to notify their doctor. If a nurse is working, tell them what's going on so they can call for help (if they're on-call). Know when to stop: Some medical emergencies are severe enough to warrant calling an ambulance. If you're injured and conscious, you should get yourself to the hospital. However, if you're severely hurt but unconscious, it may be more beneficial to save yourself for the possibility of CPR or advanced life support – especially considering that hospitals aren't always sure what level of care is necessary.

Some medical emergencies are severe enough to warrant calling an ambulance. If you're injured and conscious, you should get yourself to the hospital. However, if you're severely hurt but unconscious, it may be more beneficial to save yourself for the possibility of CPR or advanced life support – especially considering that hospitals aren't always sure what level of care is necessary. Remember to breathe: This seems obvious, but sometimes people hyperventilate and pass out.

This seems obvious, but sometimes people hyperventilate and pass out. Remember the ABCs: Any minor injuries you sustain (i.e., cuts or bruises) should be cleaned and left open to the air. Cover them with a clean cloth, pat it lightly to expand the clotting process, and look for signs of infection. For severe lacerations, apply pressure to slow blood flow until the bleeding stops. However, if there's a lot of blood, lift any nearby objects from the ground and place them beneath the wound – this will help slow blood flow long enough for you to get medical help.

Any minor injuries you sustain (i.e., cuts or bruises) should be cleaned and left open to the air. Cover them with a clean cloth, pat it lightly to expand the clotting process, and look for signs of infection. For severe lacerations, apply pressure to slow blood flow until the bleeding stops. However, if there's a lot of blood, lift any nearby objects from the ground and place them beneath the wound – this will help slow blood flow long enough for you to get medical help. Know your rights: "ER personnel is not trained in patient rights; they sometimes have task forces or emergency room consultants whose only job is to instruct the ER personnel on how to handle a medical emergency best."

If it's safe and possible, get someone else's attention who can help call an ambulance or go for help.

Try to remember what the emergency is and write it down if you can. If your mental state is impaired, try writing on your arm or hand with a marker – this will also make it easier for paramedics if they need medical records later on. If you're at home, write down the address.

Go to the nearest hospital or medical professional if you can safely do so. If there is a fire or car accident, remember that you are more likely to be injured by trying to help others than by walking away from a scary scene when there are already plenty of people on hand who can help victims.

If possible, record any information about the emergency. If you are in a car accident and the car is burning, or you have a heart attack, write down who was driving and any details such as where you live or where to start looking for other people injured or missing in case they were involved.

Keep all this information in a safe place so that it can be easily accessed if necessary, ideally marked with your name and contact details while also safely stored somewhere that will protect it from damage.

Emergencies come at different times of day and night – try not worry if you cannot get to an emergency services phone number within the first few minutes.

Knowing any medical conditions you have can be helpful in a medical emergency. Have your medications, allergies, and list of doctors ready to hand while keeping your information up to date.

If you have any valuables, consider keeping them in safes in the home, stored in a bank safe deposit box, or held at a friend's. If someone asks to look at your valuables, stick to the standard "no" responses: I'm sorry, but I don't have time to let you rummage through everything we own. What time is this? Do you know where my glasses are? If you're a victim of crime, keep a list of the emergency contacts and the police station phone number and hours that they are usually open for business.

Always let them know where you are and check up on their progress by checking with them later. If there is anyone there to help, ask if they are being given any instructions. Be honest about your physical condition and any medical conditions so that they can make an appropriate assessment of your needs or treatment.

After an emergency has finished, call the hospital or medical facility to let them know that you have arrived safely. Do not be offended if they ask why you were not there earlier.

Don't wait for someone to look for you as they may need more information than you can give at the time. It's best not to leave your name. If this is not possible, call to check with them later on.

If you have been injured, try to keep a clear head and assess the severity of your injuries. If possible, write down what happened afterward while still fresh in your memory because this will help the police or hospital staff when they ask for details. Try to stay calm – panicking will only make you feel worse, and it's more likely that you'll injure yourself further.

Please don't wait for them to find you. If you're a victim of a crime, call the police as soon as possible.

If it is safe enough, take photos of any damage that has been done and write down details about what happened while it's still fresh in your mind.

Once first responders have arrived, try to stay with them until they have finished helping. Don't leave the scene at this time – you could be in danger.

If you have been severely injured and clean sheets and blankets, consider using them to help stem the bleeding until help arrives. Make sure that they are alcohol-free, though, because rubbing alcohol can cause more damage.

If you've been injured or arrested, try to keep a clear head and remember what happened. Try to track down any witnesses and their contact details. Assess the severity of your injuries and if there are any medical conditions that you have, make sure that they are aware of them. If you have suffered property damage, get photos of it afterward (the more, the better).

It's not something we ever want to think about, but it's always a possibility. Being prepared for a medical emergency can be the difference between life and death. That's why today we're going to talk about what you can do to improve your chances of surviving a medical emergency. Let's get started!

Stay calm - being unsure or worried only widens your stress response system, which will deplete more energy from your body faster than it normally would during an emergency. Take deep breaths while you attempt to assess the situation, and don't forget to think clearly!

When trying to treat an injury on your own, remember that every situation is different depending on what type of injury it is. If you're injured, it's important to stay still and as comfortable as possible. If you are injured, make sure that you're treating the injuries appropriately - if the damage is severe enough that it could cause death, then you should seek medical attention immediately.

Once an injury has been treated, try packing the wound to prevent further contamination or infection. By plugging the damage, you're effectively stopping any water from entering the wound. If you leave the wound open, water can enter and cause an infection to grow in there. This could then lead to secondary infections and further damage.

If you should be injured while transported in a vehicle, get out immediately when it's safe to do so (if that's possible). If possible, try to sit up or move away from the vehicle as quickly as possible while still moving. This is similar to the old saying about stopping, then stepping away from a car after an accident. Depending on what you were injured by, it could be more beneficial to sit up or move away from the vehicle, but you need to use your judgment in that situation. And if you're in a medical emergency, then you should grab your kit and be prepared to treat yourself or your patient.

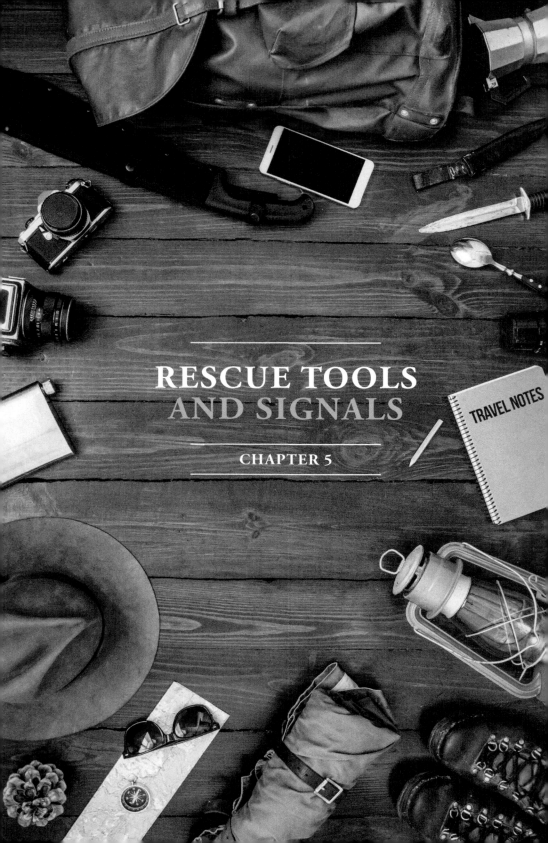

RESCUE TOOLS
AND SIGNALS

CHAPTER 5

It makes sense to be prepared in case of an emergency. Having essential survival equipment at the ready can help you survive, if not thrive, in any given situation.

- Paracord - paracord is a lightweight cord that's great for all sorts of uses, including binding objects together, making clothes, or rescuing people from dangerous situations. You need paracord if you want to be appropriately equipped to deal with any potential problem that comes up. Paracord is available in many colors and lengths, so take your pick!

- Knife - while it's not true that bad guys only come out at night, a knife still offers some level of protection during the day or night as well as when no lousy guy is present. It would help if you had a Swiss Army knife (or other multi-tool) that you can always depend on while traveling and camping.

While an air horn isn't exactly survival equipment, it's still something that can save your life.

Water Filter - water is key to living, and if you can't drink from natural water sources, you will need some way to purify the water yourself. A water filter is one of the best ways to foolproof your water source and ensures that it's safe for drinking. Handy in case you end up in a place with polluted water and also great for purifying natural water sources.

- Portable Cell Phone Charger - cell phones are great when they're charged but not so great when running out of power.

- Seasonal Clothing - this is especially important if you're going to be outside during any kind of season change. When the temperature drops, you need to dress appropriately, or else you'll freeze to death. If the temperature rises, you need to shed your layers or overheat and risk heat stroke.

- Hatchet - while not quite as versatile as a knife, the hatchet is still a great survival tool for all sorts of reasons, such as chopping wood, making shelter, and starting fires. If you don't have a hatchet, then the next best thing is a good multi-tool.

- Fire Starter - You can build a fire using wood, and once your fire is going, then it's time to use it for cooking, heating, etc... and an excellent way to start up a fire is with flint/steel, which makes ferrocerium a superb choice for your survival gear.

- Paracord Bracelets - these bracelets are great for holding things together that are likely going to come loose or where they'll get caught on other objects. Paracord is great for these purposes because it's lightweight and highly versatile.

- Survival Blanket or Sleeping Bag - this seems like something that should be obvious, but when it comes to camping, you may forget about having a sleeping bag until the night comes. A survival blanket is an excellent way to stay dry on a wet night and can serve as protection against insects or animals if there's anything at all outside. You also don't have to pack a sleeping bag if you get caught during your travels, in which case you'll be forced to do so.

- Folding Shovel - while not precisely survival gear, this is still another handy tool for redirecting water, digging holes, etc... that you should consider. You may also not carry a standard shovel, but if you can, then go for it.

- Food - this is extremely important, and if you're stranded, lost, hurt, or otherwise in a bad situation, then food will help you survive. Always bring enough food to last for however long your trip is planned to stay, plus some extra for emergencies such as being caught in the rain. Remember that your survival food needs to be light and easy to carry, so keep the amount of food at a minimum.

Water Bottle will help prevent dehydration and allow you to drink on the go

- A Good Map and Compass - being able to know where you are is extremely important, especially if help is on the way or if you're trying to navigate your way back home. If you're hiking, then make sure that you have both a good map and compass because one without the other can slow down your progress considerably.

- Energy Bars - these are a great way to gain the energy needed to hike back home if you become lost. Not only that, but they're also pretty tasty to eat.

- Credit Card and Cash - although I believe in using cash for most purchases, I tend to carry at least some credit cards for emergencies.

- Flashlight and Extra Batteries - if things go dark, then a flashlight will help immensely when lighting up dark areas.

- Pen and Paper - to note down important things such as where the person is going or why they went somewhere. A pen and paper make excellent tools for writing notes for yourself or a loved one.

- Whistle - this is a great way to get help if you're trying to call for assistance when lost. Ensure that you pack a whistle with a solid sound to attract as many people as possible.

- A water bottle - it's easy to forget things in your pack, but if you're stuck lost, a water bottle is a must. Staying hydrated is essential, too, and you'll want to keep as well-hydrated as possible to avoid dehydration. If, for some reason, you've forgotten your water bottle, make sure that you bring along another way to stay hydrated without having to stop and drink too much

- Food and Snacks - even though you might not be hungry or have much energy once you're lost, food will help. Ensure that you pack enough food such that you won't have to go out looking for food or risk getting hurt if hunger strikes at night.

- Clothing - you'll want to dress appropriately for the weather and your location, so always make sure that you have extra clothing with you. Layers are usually best as it helps control your body temperature and avoid heatstroke or hypothermia.

KNOW YOUR CITY WELL
WHERE YOU LIVE AND WORK

CHAPTER 6

You may not think that you need to know your city, or even where you live and work in it, but there are many benefits to this awareness.

The more familiar you are with the roads, buildings, landmarks and points of interest in your area, the easier it is to keep yourself safe during a disaster. Knowing the layout of your surroundings helps you find alternate routes for getting around when roads are jammed or closed due to inclement weather (allergy warning: pollen here) or flooding. Similarly, knowing where landmarks such as hospitals and police stations are located can be helpful when they're needed most — such as during an evacuation order when help in accessing these facilities is urgently required.

We live in one of the most vulnerable areas on the planet to natural disaster, and we need to be prepared.

When does your family encounter a strenuous situation?

What sorts of things might be difficult for children to handle in a strenuous situation?

What can you do to prepare your family for these types of situations?

I often find myself preparing for the unknown: traveling, camping, and going to unfamiliar places. It's hard being unfamiliar with the area or context, and it's difficult when there are people nearby who are also struggling with this. I find my best approach at making these moments less scary is through preparation.

This way, if anything is missing or I forget something, I can quickly fix it before we leave. Another idea is to pack a few extra things in your child's backpack. This way, they are prepared if they lose something on their own.

Making this process more fun for your child will make them more likely to prepare for these situations. Let them know that they will be given a treat if they keep everything organized and ready to go before leaving.

We get it. It's hard to talk about what can happen in the event of a disaster. But, if you don't prepare your family for these events now, who knows how they'll react when it happens?

This will cover all the crucial points you'll need to keep in mind when preparing your family for strenuous situations: what disasters are most likely in your area; how to assess and organize your home and property; what gear is essential for survival; and more. Plus, we'll give you some helpful guidelines on preparing children so that they're not frightened during an emergency.

Step 1: Assess And Prepare Your Home And Property

The first thing you need to do is assess the risk that your home faces from natural disasters and human-made hazards by completing these steps:

View an interactive map showing how likely each type of hazard is in your area.

Examine Your Home's Physical Features

Inspect your home's structure and assess whether it can withstand a load of a hurricane or other severe storm.

Look at your building for any weak points that may make it vulnerable to fire, floods, or earthquakes.

Examine Your Property Connected To The House

Check the pipes and power lines that connect to your home.

Review Your Insurance Policy And Other Plans

Before you make any purchases, get an insurance policy for your house. And also, consider buying extra supplies from places such as Home Depot or Amazon.com based on how likely you think you'll experience those hazards. Compare your purchase to what you need before having them delivered and ready for use.

Make sure you have emergency plans for your area.

Step 2: The Most Likely Disasters In Your Area

Next, you need to review the list of probable hazards in your area to get an idea of what disasters are most likely to happen there. For example, people in California should be more concerned about wildfires or earthquakes than flooding, while Floridians are more likely to worry about hurricanes. To help you decide what needs immediate attention and what can wait for a later time, here are some things that make each hazard more or less dangerous:

How Can You Tell If A Natural Disaster Might Affect You?

Signs Of A Hurricane Or Tornado

For a hurricane or tornado, follow these indicators for where they're headed next.

How Can You Prepare For A Tornado?

Find a place to shelter in a sturdy building.

Although this is not advisable, it's also possible to take shelter outside of your home if you can't reach a safe area.

How Can You Prepare For A Hurricane?

Even though a hurricane's strength depends on its category, powerful storms have similar, devastating effects.

Before a hurricane gets to you, make sure you know what to expect and where to get the latest news about it, including the following:

What Should People In The Path Of A Hurricane Do?

Find a shelter as soon as possible if there is no time left to evacuate. If you can't evacuate, stay inside and prepare for the worst. Have flashlights ready, as they'll become your only source of light once the power goes out. Remember that hurricanes tend to be unpredictable, so stay alert.

The Essential Gear For Survival

Besides preparing your family and property for natural disasters, you need to have the right gear so that you can all survive until help arrives.

How can you prepare for the possibility of a major earthquake in your area?

Prepare an emergency kit that's ready for when disaster strikes.

To build your kit, include the following three things: first-aid supplies, food, and water.

You can find this checklist for what else to include in your emergency kit at ready. gov.

How can you prepare for floods?

Find a safe place to live or work based on how risky your area is and do this by checking out these indicators.

If you're in a low-lying area with no high ground nearby, try to evacuate before it's too late.

How can you prepare for wildfires?

Prepare an emergency kit that's ready for when disaster strikes. To build your kit, include the following three things: first-aid supplies, food, and water.

A friend or relative can help you by stocking the emergency kit for you, but remember that they might be sick with worry while they wait for news from you.

What Should You Do In The Event Of A Nuclear Accident?

In a nuclear accident, find an area with low radiation levels or highly high-level air filters. Stay indoors until you are told to leave and always follow official instructions.

How Can You Prepare For Living In A Natural Disaster Area?

This type of preparation is made more accessible if your area's been dubbed a disaster zone.

Prepare yourself for the worst by taking the following steps:

To better evaluate what kind of equipment will be most helpful during a disaster, here's a list of things that each hazard can cause:

No matter how often you practice these safety tips, there will always be room for error. Understand that surviving is an unlikely prospect unless you seek help once it's all over. If you're lost in the woods, remember that your best chance of survival is to stay put—no straying from your route.

How Can You Prepare For An Avalanche?

The first step is to understand weather and avalanche conditions for where you're going. The third step is to prepare your equipment correctly. The fourth and final step, however, can only be learned through personal experience.

How can you prepare for extreme temperature changes?

Depending on how your body reacts with temperature changes, find a layer that works for you and pack accordingly:

Ensure your clothing layers are compatible, or they will either get in the way of one another or make it difficult to adjust as needed.

How can you prepare for heat exhaustion?

The first step in heat exhaustion is recognizing the symptoms. When it comes to heat exhaustion, four specific symptoms indicate a problem:

When heat exhaustion becomes a problem, drink water and avoid heavy exertion. Dehydration from heat and physical activity will lead to a more severe condition known as hyperthermia. If hyperthermia keeps complicating your situation, seek medical treatment immediately.

How can you prepare for swimming in severe weather?

The best way to keep yourself safe during extreme weather events is by preparing ahead of time. When it comes to swimming in severe weather, remember that water temperature can range anywhere from around 50 degrees Fahrenheit to well over 100 degrees Fahrenheit. To avoid hypothermia, make sure you wear warm clothing that will help to protect you from unforeseen.

If hypothermia becomes a problem in the water, consider floating on your back to keep your head above water. If you're not doing too much vigorous swimming, try to remember how long it's been since you've last seen land. If it's been a while, try to stay calm and conserve energy when it matters most.

Survival Skills for Children and the Elderly

If you live in a city or ever have to leave your home with nothing but what you're wearing on your back, these survival skills could save your life. Whether it's an earthquake, a 9/11-like terrorist attack, or just the next big blizzard that's touched down in the Northeast and is headed for the rest of us soon (and we all know that will happen eventually), you'll need some skills to get through it.

People often don't take the time to learn about survival skills because it might not seem necessary - but take one look at Hurricane Katrina in 2005 and tell me how wrong they are. To survive an emergency like this, there are things you should know beforehand.

The most important thing you can tell a child is this: Don't be afraid of being afraid. They shouldn't run away from the fear but rather realize it's okay to be scared and then do something about it. It's common to be afraid when you're in an uncomfortable or unfamiliar situation. Being afraid is the reason people survive in the first place. Their fear makes them take evasive action, avoid dangerous situations, and ultimately stay alive.

All of these skills are designed to save lives - especially kids'. If you don't know what to teach them, pick one and start teaching them. If you run out of time, make it a family project and teach your child how to do it with your help.

With the increase in senior care, those caring for older family members must be prepared to provide the necessities to ensure their survival.

Survival Skills for the Elderly

1) Prepare a simple meal from canned or boxed foods if possible, instead of buying expensive and fresh food.

2) Prepare a snack anytime you have a free moment, instead of spending money on fast food or full-service restaurants every time you get hungry.

3) If you have a single washer-dryer set, combine your laundry, then take it to the laundromat to save money.

4) Avoid higher calling rates by using a calling card.

5) Use long-distance telephone cards if you want to call out of state. These are excellent for getting in touch with family and friends and will save you money on your landline charges at home and reduce the cost of your long-distance service provider.

6) If you work and have childcare expenses, consider working at home if possible.

7) Re-think your transportation. For a short distance, use public transport or your own two legs instead of a car. If you do own a car, ride with friends if possible to reduce the cost of gas.

8) Look into ways to earn income at home so that you will not have to go out.

9) Use community resources in your neighborhood as much as possible to keep costs down even further.

10) If you cannot afford to cut back on your expenses, live in a cheaper home or apartment rather than renting a home or apartment.

BUGGING-IN
LONG TERM PREPARATION
CHAPTER 7

TRAVEL NOTES

It's a fact that some natural disasters can force people out of their homes: hurricanes, tornadoes, earthquakes, floods and more. And while many people return to their former lives as soon as they can — even with the knowledge that these disasters are at least somewhat predictable — others choose to "bug in" and stay put. They want to be ready for the next disaster — and bug-in for whatever comes.

Essential Equipment You Need to Survive in Any Situation, Disaster, or Emergency

It's safe to say that you never know what life will throw at you. But whatever it is, we all have the exact basic requirements for survival: shelter, food, and water, first aid. And while these are pretty straightforward necessities in every situation, a few items can help specific cases of disasters.

The Basics

This is the stuff you should have in your home and car at all times and the things you should always have in your bug-out bag. I'm going to assume that everyone knows to have a survival kit with water purification tablets, a fire starter, a whistle, a bucket of rocks, space blankets, etc. Upgrading from the basic kit is easy: just add more of what's essential for your area. You want a shawl, a few more water purification tablets, and some cheap, disposable rain suits in the South. Up North? Citronella candles and bug spray.

You also need to think about what kind of shelter items you'll need. For example, if you live in a flood-prone area and you have to evacuate quickly, it's probably not the best idea to bring your inflatable mattress with you — even though it's very comfortable! You will still need something comfortable to sleep on in your bug-out location if it's just a short evacuation.

A few other add-ons include a good set of work gloves, some way to start a fire without matches or a lighter, and the clothes you'll need to survive an extended period in the wild. Some people prefer to keep their bug-out bag at home if they need it, while others have it at their bug-out location. I think it's safest to keep your bug-out bag at your bug-out spot and stockpile some necessities for emergencies (food, water) there. You want your emergency supplies to be somewhat portable because they are limited in how long you can store them: two days is usually recommended before throwing away food and drinkable water.

Water

If you're a typical American, you think of water as a basic necessity. Think again! Water is dangerous, and it can be challenging to find. Some cities don't even have running water, and most towns don't offer potable water 24/7. Depending on what area you need to bug out in, it could take hours for authorities to get to your emergency location. In short, you need clean drinking water in an emergency.

It's hard enough finding clean tap water when it's not contaminated because of sewage backups or other unknown factors — let alone in the middle of an emergency! Even if you find fresh water, it might not be safe to drink without filtering it first. So, where is clean water? In your toilet tank. Most homes have a reserve of water in the toilet tank, and that water is usually fresh and clean.

If there's a situation where you won't have access to water in your toilet tank (the house has been destroyed, for example), you can always use survival straws. Most restaurants use them to serve water, and they last for months.

Food

Most disaster experts recommend packing about a one-month supply of food in your bug-out bag. Again, the problem with finding food is that there are too many variables: the type of terrain you are navigating through, how many people need to be fed in the area, how much water is available, how long it will take authorities to get there — the list goes on.

The first is an MRE, or "Meal Ready to Eat" — they're usually pretty easy to find, and what's more, they can last for years if they're stored in the right conditions. MREs come with their containers, so everything is self-contained and easy to transport. But even though MREs are excellent, you don't need them — most survivalists say that you can live solely off of eating canned food for an extended period (just make sure it's from a can that isn't swollen). You can also just buy some canned food in the store if it's necessary, but you may not have it available when you need it.

The second thing I recommend is a backup water filter that can be used for several months without a problem (so long as there's clean water, to begin with). These filters are great because instead of carrying several bottles of water with you, one filter lasts for up to two months. Also, don't forget to include a good set of water purification tablets in your bag as well. These will help you purify and disinfect any water you do find, so you don't have to worry about things like giardia and other nasty stuff.

HOME
DEFENCE

CHAPTER 8

How To Protect the Family?

If you're looking for self-defense and survival tips, you've come to the right place. Our goal is to provide solutions for everything from escape a bear attack to defend yourself against a group assault situation.

So here are some tips on self-defense and survival:

1) If an opponent is more significant than you, run away from them – they'll most likely just chase you down. This is called "The Bigger They Are, The Harder They Fall." You can also use weapons and vehicles to your advantage too.

2) If an opponent is more robust than you, use weapons like handguns or knives instead of fighting them directly. Weapons are called the "great equalizer" because they can level the playing field between bigger and stronger opponents.

3) If an opponent is in a group, run away or call the police. Most likely, you'll get hurt if you try to fight them off directly. As we mentioned before, weapons are mighty in a situation like this to help keep all of your attackers at bay at one time.

4) If you're pulled over for a traffic violation, keep your cool. Just hand over your registration and put it in the ignition, and just do it.

5) If you have a gun or knife, always have extra ammunition on hand. Also, practice shooting your weapon at least once each year to ensure it's still working correctly.

6) Keep a sharp eye out for trouble at night, especially if you're walking around alone or in an unfamiliar place.

7) Know how to defend yourself in everyday situations, such as a bar fight. If you're sober enough, it's best just to walk away and not get involved with people like this. If you can't run away, then here's how you should proceed: use the bar stools you have around you or even the chairs from a table to help keep your distance from them. Use table legs and other long objects as weapons if necessary. When they get close, hit them hard and repeatedly in their stomach.

8) Don't wear earphones in public places – this way, you can be more aware of what's happening around you at all times.

9) Always carry your ID in your wallet or purse at all times – this way, if you're arrested, you can prove who you are and contact an attorney.

10) If someone follows you in a car, try to find somewhere to hide if there isn't anywhere to hide and look for your transportation.

Community Relations

Urban survival is a difficult endeavor. It requires a range of skills and abilities to be successful. Depending on your goals, they can include everything from day-to-day living and self-sufficient living off the land to urban combat and long term navigation of unfamiliar areas in search of resources. The long-term nature of many aspects of this life means it is important for communities to work together and develop sustainable practices for the future. Communities can learn from each other just as much as individuals within the community, but before that can happen there must be some level of trust established among members so that members will share information with each other without fear or shame.

Respect is important because without it you can never gain allies, let alone friends. Your community should be more than a group of friends or people who are generally tolerant of each other. Every member should have the right to speak their opinion on any given matter. Individual wants and needs should not be kept hidden from the group, but they need to be tempered or adjusted in order to promote general harmony among the group. A good leader must have these skills as well as an understanding of how other people work for them to set an example for others.

Even if people have the right to speak their mind, they should avoid offending others in the group when doing so. If you disagree with someone, it is important to do so in a respectful manner that doesn't belittle their opinions.

Your reputation is your most important asset within any community. Be known for your strengths and make others forget about your weaknesses as best you can. Build up trust among community members by keeping your word and being reliable as a source of information and support. By cultivating such a reputation, you will be able to both ask favors of other people and gain their support when needed.

Ideally, your reputation should precede you anywhere you go. Your name and face should instill a sense of respect and maybe even a modicum of fear. If people have heard good things about you and know that they are safe around you, it will make it easier to gain their trust and cooperation when needed. On the other side of that coin, if people have heard bad things about you, be prepared to live up to that reputation or work hard to overcome those preconceived notions of your personality. This is not the sort of thing you can fake either, as it takes time to build this kind of reputation among your peers.

CONCLUSION

If you're like me, you know how important it is to have a disaster plan for your family. The unfortunate truth is that disasters can strike at any time, and when they do, the best of us can easily be undone. Follow these steps to get ready for the worst and to increase your odds of coming out unscathed:

1) Assemble an emergency kit that includes everything from food and water for three days to an extra set of keys with batteries and phone chargers. Keep a copy in the car as well as one at home, so they're accessible no matter where you are if disaster strikes.

2) Create a family emergency plan that outlines a course of action in the event of an emergency or natural disaster.

3) Identify safe places to go and people to contact. Ensure your whole family is prepared to leave the "box" in case you need to evacuate. You should also consider relocating away from high-risk areas, like flood zones, and acquiring long-term supplies like water, batteries for radios and flashlights, food for home cooking, and canned food packed in durable containers that are easy to move.

4) Always stay informed, especially on stormy days. Check out NOAA's Weather Radio by clicking here. You can also sign up for the news service on the radio too.

5) Update your family's health insurance policies and check on travel and evacuation plans.

6) Contact local officials to see how they can be of assistance. Many times, local officials will provide evacuations or sheltering services based on needs. Do not hesitate to call your county's emergency management office or 911 if you need assistance during an emergency (or any other time!)

7) Have a Plan B in place. Having one is critical when disaster strikes; it can make the difference between life and death if you cannot contact your family members because of power outages or cell phone towers down.

8) If you are going to evacuate, secure your family members and pets, especially those who have health problems or are young/infirm. Make sure a list of names and phone numbers for everyone is available in case of an emergency.

9) Practice your role as coordinator of family duties during an emergency or disaster. Not everyone will have time to run out the door, get gas and snacks for everyone or buy extra supplies.

10) Have a cash supply on hand at home in case banks and ATMs are not operational.

11) Keep your family safe by making sure everyone knows what to do in the event of an emergency outside the home – like when you're at work or school, for example.

Take every precaution to ensure that no matter what happens, you are ready to handle it. I've assembled this intending to help you be as prepared as possible for any disaster – big or small.

Once you have your list together, prioritize it according to importance. It should be pretty straightforward at this point since there's nothing on your list that isn't necessary for survival in these circumstances... However, there is no harm in prioritizing based on what's most convenient or what will last for an emergency.

The following steps are more difficult without having any practical experience (we're sorry!). Try to determine how much (or how little) you'll need each item on your list at a time. Remember that you can't store unlimited amounts of food or water.

Some things, like matches or medicines, are more vital than others. Think about what would happen if there were no supplies for these items and what that would mean for your survival should an apocalyptic event occur now...

Once you've made your list, you should make up a rotating system for your survival supplies. Decide what to store where and how often the items on your list should be rotated to make sure they're always fresh. You'll also need to decide how many of each item you're going to store. The best way to do this is by making a chart or a graph.

If your supplies are limited, remember that it's better to have some food in storage than none at all.

After you've decided what items to store, put them in a backpack or other container and place them in a secure area. Now that your list is complete and your supplies have been prioritized, it's time to move on to the next step.

Also, remember to keep your supplies from getting damaged or soaked by water. Water - especially if it's coming in after an earthquake - is very destructive to most things made of metal and plastic. You don't want something fundamental like a flashlight or batteries to get ruined because someone has forgotten about his emergency supplies... So be sure to keep them dry and well protected from the elements.

Before you leave for your vacation, take care of some of these preparations so that when you get back home, you'll be ready for whatever disaster may come your way.

To prepare your community for a disaster, you will need to:

Plan for the best possible outcome, but also plan for and prepare for the worst. Prepare at every level of government, including the Federal Emergency Management Agency (FEMA). Become knowledgeable of local emergency procedures. Be prepared to follow those procedures effectively in the event of an emergency. Be ready to assist others who may be unable to do so themselves.

When a natural disaster strikes, people need to know where they can turn for assistance. They need to know what steps to take to save their own lives. They need to know how to keep their families safe and what they should do if faced with the aftermath of the disaster. People need to be informed and ready - because, in the end, preparation truly is the key.

Since 1980, over 100 million Americans have participated in preparedness activities sponsored by FEMA, with more than 100 million people participating annually. FEMA's preparedness activities include public information campaigns, local emergency planning committees, community emergency exercises, and many other activities designed to increase individual and community preparedness for disasters.

It is essential to realize that the emergency preparedness activity sponsored by FEMA is not an endorsement of any particular product, company, or strategy. Participating in preparedness activities does not imply your agreement with or endorsement of any specific plans, programs, or products that may be mentioned.

This is about preparing for disaster and some everyday things that people do wrong during disasters that make them stay unsafe longer than they would without those misconceptions.

The reason why it is bad for you and your family or co-workers not to panic and attempt to run away from the area is that if others are panicking also, then there can be accidents occurring that could injure many others at one time where only one or two injuries would have been if everyone stayed calm.

If possible, it is also essential to avoid driving during a disaster. Not only can the roads be damaged due to cars and trucks getting in accidents, but many people who abandon their vehicles can be killed by nearby traffic if they are hit by another car. When you decide to drive anyway, make sure that you don't take any unnecessary risks or that there will be no other vehicles on the road. Also, stay off the highways unless necessary, especially public transit systems where there may be a higher chance of an accident or terror attack.

Another thing to keep in mind is that when available, make sure to have an emergency kit with you that includes items such as flashlights, batteries, a battery-powered radio, food, and water for at least two weeks, medicines and first-aid supplies, and protection (such as a firearm or non-lethal weapon) for each member of your family. Also, make sure to have someone outside of the area that can be reached quickly in case of an emergency.

Remember this: many disaster situations occur at night when the public isn't able to see what is going on very well. You may find that you and your family are in danger when you are out during the day and in the dark. It is vital to stay alert during the day as well.

Despite many people thinking it's best to have a shower after being at a disaster site, there are many reasons why this particular type of activity is not suitable for everyone or for everyone at the same time. First, there is a chance of contamination from plants or water supplies directly after a disaster occurs, especially if there is flooding or other chemical spills that can happen. Second, there are dangers of drowning or falling in the shower, such as getting out of the storm. Third, when you're at a disaster site and don't have electricity, batteries would be impossible.

If someone is injured and bleeding because they had an accident at a disaster scene or elsewhere, it's essential to make sure they are taken to a proper location right away for emergency care. You also don't want to over-use first-aid items that are available such as gauze and bandages, if more advanced help is needed.

News media have many responsibilities and should be able to broadcast what is going on at the time of a disaster. This can be extremely important because it will let everyone know that help is on the way or what they need to do in case of an emergency. Television news shows worldwide are beneficial because they will explain how to stay safe during a natural disaster. This is especially true because many children are glued to their television sets during disaster-related shows so that they know what's going on.

If you're in charge of any organization like your local school, you should plan for the worst-case scenario. Sometimes this is announced before the disaster occurs, and sometimes the information comes out after. If you don't have this type of training, you'll be blindsided by the tragedy as well.

The best time to prepare for a natural disaster or other situation is when it doesn't seem like there will be one at all. The more time that goes by without a major catastrophe, the harder it will be to adjust your plans to accommodate it when it does happen.

This focuses on why we should be prepared and what we can do to prepare ourselves for a natural or human-made disaster.

This information is not available to the general public when it comes to catastrophe, so we need to find out what we can do to prepare ourselves for a natural or human-made disaster.

You can do the two most important things if you know that there will be a disaster: first, having an emergency kit and staying away from dangerous areas.

You can also put other things in your emergency kits such as money, medicine, food, and water for at least two weeks, as well as protection (such as a firearm or non-lethal weapon) for each member of your family. Also, make sure to have someone outside of the area that can be reached quickly in case of an emergency.

The time between disaster events varies from person to person because it depends on the earthquake or storm about to hit and what type of disaster will be happening.

Sometimes disasters are expected but not always.

There are many tips when dealing with a disaster, and knowing what to do will help you stay safe. This is very important because we need to know what the situation is going on to prepare for it properly. Keep your emergency kit handy at all times, as well as learning what everyone needs in case one of these situations occurs in the future.

Hopefully, you will never have to use your disaster kit, but it is always good to be prepared.

BOOK 2
OUTDOOR
SURVIVAL

INTRODUCTION

Staying calm is the first thing to do in order to survive in the wilderness is stay calm.

You're probably wondering, "what should I do?" That's a good question, but it's not as simple as just answering it.

"Reasonability" is a key factor for many wilderness survival scenarios.

A general rule of thumb is that you should try and stay as close to the ground as possible when in the outdoors.

If you are stranded in a tree house or on a mountain peak, it is generally safe to descend every so often in order to relieve yourself. Your tree house probably won't survive being knocked down by an overzealous rhino, so be cautious when doing so – but if it does survive, then again, keep your cool! You'll want to check yourself over and make sure that nothing was broken during the fall – but don't panic if you don't spot anything.

Sometimes, it can be useful to stay in a tree for long periods of time.

You might be able to store extra water in the tree's hollow base.

If you're in a ravine (such as those found in the forests of Idaho) or a canyon, it might not be wise to climb up every few hours and check on other survival supplies. It is more important that you stay calm and conserve your energy – when others come looking for you, you'll want to look as best as possible without being conspicuous.

It's a good idea to stay in the same general area that you were dumped in. If you're lucky and were dumped at the entrance of an abandoned mineshaft, you might want to think about sticking close to it, but move carefully as it could be mined.

It is also possible to use your emergency supplies to create homemade shelters. This is a good way of keeping yourself warm without any need for fire. You can put leaves on a bed of dry grass and sleep underneath them (or shelter under your own makeshift lean-to).

It is also useful to train yourself on how to create simple tools and weapons out of the resources that you have in your immediate environment. You might be able to make a simple hatchet out of a broken branch or bend a tree branch into something resembling a spear. Many trees, especially ones with soft wood, can resist breaking – so if you're going for this option, you might want to test it before attempting it on your own life-tree.

'Tree-knives' are one of the most primitive weapons that a survivor could create – they are made from sharpening the bark from around the tree so that it resembles some sort of handle grip. They were used by Native Americans for hunting and protection.

It is also extremely important that you keep a level head and be able to think clearly during your time in the wilderness – it could really be the difference between life and death.

It has been stated that unless you have survived the elements of nature, you are not really equipped to withstand any tragedy. When exposed to certain extremes, the human body is fragile and will only be able to resist them for a short period of time before breaking down. In this chapter, you will learn how to defend yourself from some of the factors discussed in the previous chapter. It is vital to remember that some of these survival strategies are not intended to be used for lengthy periods of time in high temperatures. Furthermore, if you find yourself trapped without the necessary tools or supplies, there isn't much you can do to remedy the situation. As a result, it is critical to seek refuge in a secure location and remain there until relief arrives.

BUGGING-OUT
CREATE AN EVACUATION PLAN

CHAPTER 1

Prepare for the worst with these disaster prevention tips!

It's not always easy to predict natural disasters, but thankfully there are ways to minimize your risk of them happening. From preparing an emergency kit to making sure you know how your home is insured, these disaster prevention tips will ensure you're ready in the event of a disaster.

It's essential to be prepared for a disaster in your area. Disasters are unpredictable and can strike at any time. But being prepared can help you avoid or minimize the effects of a disaster.

Find out if there is an evacuation route from where you live, work, or study that doesn't pass under trees or over hills during heavy storms.

Don't forget to plan for safety and comfort in the absence of electricity

Make a family emergency evacuation plan

Know where your neighbors live, work, or study so you can help them if they are in need.

Fill up your gas tank before a significant storm so you won't be left with a severe shortage of fuel afterward.

If you work in or near a school, learn what to do if there is a threat of an active shooter.

Check for gas leaks before a storm is about to hit or during the shower at your home, business, or place of worship if that's where you're providing emergency services. This will prevent fires from destroying homes and businesses.

Avoid overloading extension cords and appliances with heavy loads like clothes and furniture; they can cause fires if they get caught in a nearby wall heater, portable heater, or another device.

Put away anything that can burn at least six feet above the floor: fireplaces and logs, flower pots, stoves, grills, outdoor heaters, and other appliances.

Increase the distance from tall buildings. If you live in a high-rise building, stay in your building if it is safe to do so. Take the stairs unless an alternate object will prevent you from falling, such as a railing.

Make sure your home has fire extinguishers, especially ones that can be used indoors.

Has an emergency kit packed and ready for use at all times? Your equipment should have a battery-powered or hand-crank radio, extra flashlights and batteries, a first aid kit, food, water, and additional medication.

Batteries, Emergency Candles, and Lighters

The emergency preparedness industry has been booming for the last few years, and rightfully so. Have you taken your disaster prep seriously? If not, it's time to get prepared—the following list of items is perfect for any emergency kit.

Lighters: These products are commonly used in both high-tech and low-tech ways. You could use them to light an oil lamp or candle, start a campfire, or control sparks from flint and steel. These items should be kept in the house or car for your safety.

Flashlights: These products provide light at night and are often used for additions to camping gear. They can also be used in emergencies, such as when you are lost in the dark and need to find a way back home.

Batteries: Batteries are a necessity for various electronics, ranging from flashlights to radios.

Food: Food is necessary to live and survive during an emergency, so ensure that you have enough food on hand for your family's needs. Keep three to five days of food in your kit at all times, regardless of what the stores are selling.

Water: Ensure that you know how to purify water as well as making it healthy for drinking.

First Aid Supplies: You should always have a first aid kit on hand for any sort of emergencies that might occur, both large and small. Ensure that you can provide care for primary injuries such as stitches or burns.

Emergency Medication: If necessary, you should also have enough medication on hand that can treat minor illnesses. This should include medicines such as painkillers and aspirin. Extra packing tape for both first aid and medical use is also needed.

It's true—disasters have a way of sneaking up on us without warning, but it's never too early to get prepared!

Pack a Back-Up Just in Case!

Bug-out-Bag

Bug-Out Bag Checklist

When it comes to setting up your bug-out bag, there are several different things that you will need. First, you need to gather all the essentials that you'll need to survive. If you decide to make your own bug-out bag, then you'll have to do some research on what items are available for sale and what items can help you survive the crisis. If you do not have enough money right now to buy each item at once, then it's best if you budget yourself so that you can get everything that's on your list as soon as possible.

Things To Consider For Your Checklist

Hydration (H2O)—This is one of the most valuable things that anyone would want during an evacuation. It's important that you have plenty of water at hand just in case the lack of it causes you to become dehydrated. When the time comes, you'll want to have your own personal supply of water and purification equipment available for quick relief. To ensure that your water supply is safe, make sure it meets all safety measures.

Hygiene—keeping yourself clean can be a challenge during an emergency. What would you do if there is no running water or a public restroom? Along with toiletries, it's best if you have a way of disposing of any bodily waste when there are no other options left on hand.

Knives—you'll be needing to cut things, and you'll need to do it quickly. A good quality utility knife will do just fine and is likely better than any other kind of knife you might have in your home. Having spare blades on hand will also ensure that you're able to make clean cuts and prevent splinters in the process.

Lighters—if you ran out of matches or use a lighter on a regular basis, it's likely that your emergency stash should have some on hand as well.

Pepper spray—pepper spray is an excellent self-defense option when it comes to protecting yourself against intruders who may be planning on robbing you. It's best that this is a chemical spray in case it becomes necessary to defend yourself with the substance. Make sure that this goes inside your bag so you can carry it, just in case an intruder breaks into your home while you're away.

Plastic bags—keep some plastic bags on hand in case you have to use the restroom. You may not want to use one of the bags for everything, but it's best that you have a small amount of each available for when you can't hold it.

Sabers or shaving razors—you'll need to shave often during an evacuation, and having a good quality razor available will ensure that you look great while you go through your emergency preparations. You can also use this as a weapon if necessary and grab them when they are not in use.

Shovels—in case you have to break through walls or dig through dirt, a shovel will help you get through it. It's best to have a good quality solid steel shovel and keep it clean so that it's ready for whenever you might need to use it. Shovel is one of the best and most useful items that you can keep on hand during an emergency.

Shelter —you'll want some sort of shelter in case you need to stay somewhere else during an emergency. You'll be able to take shelter in a tree, bush, or even under your car where possible. It's best to consider your location before you pack anything for shelter. Make sure that you have enough space to not feel claustrophobic and completely protected from the elements until it's safe to go home again.

Toiletries—you need to keep yourself clean when going through an emergency. Aside from toilet paper and soap, it's a good idea to have plenty of other items on hand as well, just in case. Make sure that your emergency bug-out bag has a variety of personal care products available for when the time comes.

BOB Checklist

- Bag or box.

- Twelve months' supply of food and water (shouldn't need to go more than two in an emergency).

- Four sources of potable water for up to five people over a one-week period.

- Two food sources per person of at least twelve-month storage from your food storage plan and two additional sources per person in case one source is compromised. This should provide enough food for one week in the event it goes bad. This will allow your family member the ability to get by using what they already have or can buy with what little money they have left. Consider purchasing freeze dried meat, fish, superfoods, etc., in bulk and storing in a variety of containers.

- Two sources of potable water for one week.

- Three-month supply of medications.

Tools

- One flashlight with batteries and extra bulbs.

- A hand-cranked or solar-powered radio or lantern for communication over long distances, including shortwave bands if opposed to FM and AM broadcast transmissions. Ensure that it is weatherproof and built-in battery or crank. These are essential to use as your primary source of light since they are often the only means by which you can communicate outside during an emergency besides shouting, which can be difficult to do when out in the woods. They can also be used as an alarm, signaling someone nearby with an SOS calling signal.

- Four batteries and an extra power pack.

- A signal mirror or signal panel with a bright background.

- A whistle with lanyard, which can be used to signal for help. You should also have a secondary method of signaling that is not dependent on the environment and will work even if you are wet, sleepy or otherwise incapacitated. This could include emergency flares and floating devices or smoke signals. Anything that will let people find you when it's needed.

- Two emergency blankets. This is your portable shelter for cold weather situations. This should fit into every BOB and go bag, even into your car. If you don't have a space for it at home or vehicle, then get creative by carrying it in a stuff sack or pillowcase. Ensure that you have enough to last at least two days for each person.

- Two emergency sleeping bags.

- You need a waterproof tarp with grommets to put over your BOB or go bag to protect it from the elements. You can also use this as a ground covering and place it under your tent to keep out water and debris.

- One set of lighter, waterproof matches, and waterproof fire starter.

- A first-aid kit having at least a small medical reference book, a good quality first-aid manual, sanitized dressings and bandages, disinfectant, insect repellant, antihistamines (for bites and stings), antiseptics (for cleaning wounds), tweezers, scissors, safety pins or shears for cutting bandages (if needed), paracord or string to place around your BOB to keep items from getting lost and also for multiple uses such as hanging your bag or tent.

- Good-quality fixed blade knife. At least three feet of 550 paracord, or parachute cord. A compass with protractor and map of the area, preferably waterproof.

- Multifunctional tool (knife, pliers, serrated blade, can opener, screwdrivers).

- Whistle or signal mirror.

- A self-defense weapon such as a handgun or pocket knife

- Matches or waterproof fire starters.

Mistakes To Avoid With BOB

You don't want to be in a situation where SHTF and you find yourself with nothing to rely on other than what you have with you. That's why it's important to make sure your BOB is well-stocked.

Here are our top mistakes to avoid when packing a bug-out bag:

1) Too Many Gear Items: A bug-out bag should only contain essentials that serve multiple purposes. If there is too much gear in your BOB, chances are it will be too heavy or cumbersome for any quest longer than an hour without needing re-connaissance (aka wasting precious time).

2) Items Not Necessary: Some people pack items that are not necessary for survival, but more for bragging rights and to establish their "prowess" in the field. While this may help them appear more experienced in the eyes of others, it makes them less prepared to face any situation. Bug-out bags should be small enough so that you can carry them with your hands (no backpacks). If you are going to use a backpack, pack it light and leave out items that serve no purpose.

3) No Food Or Water: One of the most important things in a survival situation is food. You burn approximately 2000cal per day just living. You NEED food to survive. Make sure your BOB contains high caloric foods such as nuts and raisins so that you have energy to get through the worst case scenario SHTF. Next, make sure your BOB has at least one gallon of water per person to last 3 days (3L water per day per person). If you live in a hot climate, increase this amount by 50%.

4) No Shelter: Shelter is important to save your life from the elements and keep you hidden from other humans. Make sure your BOB has a lightweight tarp or tent that is easily concealable.

5) No Fire Starter: Starting a fire is one of the most important things in a survival situation and something you cannot live without. Make sure your BOB has waterproof matches, candles, match-sticks, lighters or some type of flint (serrated knife, magnesium block with striker, etc.).

6) No Weapons: The chances are slim that at some point during a long-term bug-

out you will run into other humans who have either lost their way or have sinister intentions. Make sure your BOB has a small knife (fixed blade, not folding), multiple throwing knives and a gun of some sort.

7) No Communication: Make sure your BOB has compact walkie-talkie(s), cell phone or hand cranked radio so that you can maintain communication with other members of your group.

8) No Documentation: Make sure the BOB has waterproof documents such as maps, directions, other contact info and anything else related to the case scenario.

Use the fact that no one will be there to help you out in this situation to prepare your most important tool: Your mind.

By following this guide and taking the time to prepare your bug-out backpack, you can rest assured that in the case of an emergency, you will be well prepared for survival.

ORIENTATION

CHAPTER 2

Today, almost everyone has access to a GPS navigation system, whether it's the GPS mounted in your car or Google Maps on your phone. Not many even own a physical map anymore; electronic gadgets have become the go-to way of traveling. Whenever you need to go somewhere and you're not sure about how to get there, you simply plug the coordinates or address into your GPS and off you go.

Most people have lost the ability or have never learned the skill necessary to orient themselves and travel without the help of technology. However, when you get yourself turned around and lost in the wilderness, whether you're spending time outdoors recreationally or find yourself in an emergency situation, technology may not be able to help you. Your battery may run flat or there may not be sufficient signal for your GPS to work. In these circumstances, you need to know how to use your surroundings to find your way back to civilization.

Compass and Map

The most basic navigation and orienteering tools everyone should have in a survival backpack are a map of the area you are going to be in and a reliable compass. It's essential to have an up-to-date map of the specific area you are in. If you are spending time outdoors away from home, a map of your home town or city isn't going to be of much use. Likewise, not all compasses are created equal and it's worthwhile investing in a quality compass that won't leave you in the lurch when you really need it.

Orientation on Arrival

When you arrive in a new wilderness area for recreational purposes, it's important that you orient yourself before you do anything else. You should figure out and make note of where your vehicle, campsite, the entrance to a hiking trail, and the nearest road or town is. That way, if you do get lost, you will know which direction you need to travel in. When you're lost, it's imperative to know which way you should go; otherwise, you could spend precious time, even days, walking without reaching help.

Natural Directional Cues

There are several ways you can determine direction in the wilderness using your surroundings, from the sun and shadows to the night sky and even rudimentary natural compasses or a watch.

Sun and Shadows

The sun rises in the east and sets in the west, or so we think. The fact is that it's not exactly due west or east. The movement of the sun is also affected by seasonal variations. Despite all of this, you can still utilize it to determine direction.

Northern hemisphere: At noon, when the sun is at its highest point in the sky and casts almost no shadows, the sun will be due south.

Southern hemisphere: At noon when the sun is highest, it will be due north.

Shadow-Tip Methods for Direction

Method One

The first of the two methods is accurate and relatively simple to use. It requires you to find a one-meter long straight stick. You will also need to find a level patch of ground that is clear of vegetation so your stick can cast a decent shadow.

☒ Observe the direction in which the sun rose or the direction it's moving in. Rising in the east and setting in the west. This will give you an approximation of which way is east and which way is west.

☒ Place your stick into the ground in your clear, level spot.

☒ Mark the sport where the tip of the shadow falls on the ground with a twig, stone, or another item that won't blow away.

☒ Everywhere in the world, this first shadow-tip marking always runs in an east-west line. So, one end of the shadow line will be facing east and the other end will be facing west. Which direction the tip of the shadow is facing is determined by the time of day.

☒ Since the sun rises in the east, using the morning sun, the tip of the shadow will point towards the west. As the sun travels west in the afternoon, the top of the shadow will be pointing east.

☒ Once you have marked the first shadow-tip, wait about 10 to 15 minutes. The shadow tip will move as the sun moves overhead. After waiting a while, mark where the second shadow-tip falls on the ground just as you did with the first one.

☒ Remembering the general direction the sun rose in being east, point your left hand east. Stand with one foot on each mark so your left hand is still pointing east. You are now facing the general direction of true north.

Method Two

The alternative shadow-tip method is more accurate than the first one but takes longer to complete.

☒ As with the first method, find a one-meter long straight stick and place it onto the ground in a clear, level area. Do this step in the morning.

☒ At midday, the stick will cast almost no shadow at all and the shadow will gradually begin to lengthen again as the afternoon wears on.

☒ During the afternoon, mark where the second shadow-tip falls and draw a line to connect the marks. The first mark will indicate east and the second mark will indicate west. Stand on the line with west on your left side and east on your right; north will be in front of you.

Moon and Stars

Using the sun and the shadows it casts can help you determine direction during the day. The moon and stars in the night sky can help you determine direction during the night. Knowing how to employ both methods of finding direction will allow you to find your bearings at any time of the day or night.

Moon

The only time we can see the moon is when it's reflecting the light of the sun. The moon orbits the earth in a 28-day cycle during which time the shape and side of the moon the light is on changes in accordance with its position relative to earth.

When there is no moon or a new moon, the moon and sun are on opposite sides of the earth. As the moon moves out of the shadow the earth casts on it, the moon is said to be waxing as it gets fuller. As the moon moves back into the earth's shadow, it's said to be waning as it gets smaller again. You can use the side of the moon that reflects sunlight to determine direction.

At moonrise, if the sun has not yet set, the side of the moon reflecting light will indicate west. If the moon only rises after midnight, the side reflecting light will indicate east. This will give you a rough idea of the west-east line. Standing with west on your left and east on your right, north will be in front of you.

Stars

The constellations used to determine north or south differ between the northern and southern hemispheres.

Northern Hemisphere

The constellations you need to learn to accurately and easily identify in the northern hemisphere are the Big Dipper, also known as the Ursa Major or Plow, and Cassiopeia. Both of these constellations are always visible when the weather at night is clear and the stars are visible. You will use these two constellations to locate the North Star, also known as Polaris or the polestar.

The North Star makes up part of the handle of the Little Dipper, which can be confused with the Big Dipper. Avoid this confusion by using both Cassiopeia and the Big Dipper to determine the North Star. These two constellations are always located exactly opposite each other. The North Star is in the center of them and the two constellations rotate in a counterclockwise direction around it.

The Big Dipper can be identified as a constellation made up of seven stars with the two stars that make up the outer edge of the dipper bucket pointing towards the North Star. The distance between these two pointer stars is approximately ⊠ of the length between the last dipper bucket star and the North Star. Use your imagination to draw a line five times the length between the start in the direction they are pointing to find the North Star. The position of the North Star will provide you with an idea of where north is.

Southern Hemisphere

In the southern hemisphere, you are going to use the Southern Cross, or Crux, to determine where south is. This constellation is made up of four stars that if you draw lines between them will form a cross that is tilted to one side. The two stars that make up the long axis of the constellation are used as pointer stars. Mentally draw a line in the same direction as the two pointer stars that is five times the distance between them and mark an imaginary point. At this point, drop a line straight down to the horizon and this will indicate a general southern direction.

Using a Watch

To use a watch to determine direction, you need to have an analog watch or a watch that has hands to tell the time. Your watch also has to be set to the true local time of the area you are in. Make sure your watch is not set for daylight savings time. To use a watch that is set for daylight saving, see an explanation below. It's also useful to keep in mind that the closer to the equator you are, the less accurate this method is. The further from the equator you are, the more accurate it will be.

Northern hemisphere: Hold your watch horizontal or parallel to the ground. Point the hour hand of your watch at the sun. Observe where the 12 0'clock mark is on your watch face. Take note of the point exactly in the middle between your hour hand that is facing the sun and your 12 o'clock mark.

Southern hemisphere: Hold your watch horizontal or parallel to the ground. Point the 12 o'clock mark of your watch at the sun. Observe where the hour hand is pointing on your watch face. Take note of the point exactly in the middle between your 12 o'clock mark that is facing the sun and your hour hand.

The midpoint between your hour hand and the 12 o'clock mark will indicate the north-south line. At noon, the sun will be due north. If you have any doubts as to which side of the line is north and which is south, remember that the sun rises in the east and sets in the west.

Daylight Saving: If you have your watch set to daylight saving time, adjust the above method. Instead of using the hour hand and the 12 o'clock mark on your watch, use the hour hand and the 1 o'clock mark and note the midpoint between the two as above.

Moss

Contrary to popular belief, moss does not only grow on one side of trees; it often grows all the way around a tree. However, the growth of moss will be more prolific and lush on the side of a tree that faces away from the equator. In the northern hemisphere, this will be on the north side, and in the southern hemisphere, it will be on the south side. It's helpful to use several trees for comparison to more accurately determine direction.

Streams and Rivers

Streams and rivers may not help you determine direction but they are a useful navigation tool when you're out in the wilderness, whether you're just hiking or find yourself lost. You can easily follow the course of a stream or river, which will guide you downhill, often towards a larger body of water such as a lake. Although they twist and turn along their route, you won't end up going in circles, which is helpful in conserving vital energy if you're lost. Providing they aren't polluted or stagnant, you can also use rivers and streams as a source of water along the way. This conserves energy and resources you would otherwise have to expend searching for water sources in the outdoors.

When in Doubt

Finding yourself in an emergency situation or lost in the wilderness can be a dangerous situation. Even more dangerous is trying to find your way out of the wild if you don't have the knowledge, skills, and experience to make your way to safety. Trying to find your own way back to civilization presents many risks, such as becoming even more lost or having an accident. These risks could well turn out to be life-threatening in these kinds of situations. If there is someone who knows the general area you were in and reports you missing, it's best to stop moving and stay where you are. Once a search begins, moving around could be very disruptive to those rescue efforts. Staying in one place will help any search and rescue efforts locate and rescue you more easily and quickly. You can employ your survival and bushcraft skills (**Bushcraft** is the art of wilderness survival using traditional skills and knowledge in the natural environment) to keep you alive while you wait for help.

BUILDING A
SAFE HAVEN

CHAPTER 3

How to Make an Emergency Shelter for Survival Situations

If you find yourself out in the wilderness, away from any sign of civilization, you'll want to have a plan for sheltering yourself. This provides step-by-step instructions on constructing one of the most basic and effective shelters — the lean-to.

It can easily be made with minimal tools and supplies and is an excellent way to keep warm in cold weather settings.

The shelter can be made using only one 50ft long flexible tree branch (4ft in diameter), 3 or 4 short, sturdy tree branches (1" diameter), two plastic tarps, rope, twine, and five extra foot square of carpeting or tarp for an area rug.

Step 1: Start by finding a clearing in a forest or meadow, with enough room for your lean-to and space for a fire. If you're building your shelter in the woods, make sure the site is clear of dead branches and other debris that could accidentally start a fire.

Step 2: Find two trees about 8ft apart. One tree should be straight and about 10 feet tall, and the other should be flexible enough to bend over from its base towards the ground at an angle of 45 degrees. These two trees will support all of the weight of the lean-to, so they must be strong enough to hold it up.

Step 3: Next, tie the arch tree to one end of the ridge beam using a rope or twine long enough to wrap around both trees.

Use 1-inch nylon rope. It won't seep moisture into your lean-to, and it's solid and lightweight to carry into the wilderness.

Step 4: Use a knife to cut many flexible branches you can use as horizontal support beams for your shelter. Then lash them together using some kind of twine or rope. These will support the tarp roof, so they need to be strong – that's why you should use branches with a diameter of at least an inch.

Step 5: Find a short, sturdy branch that you can use as a ridge pole for the roof. Then tie the end of your ridge pole to the arch tree.

Ridge poles should be at least 6-8 feet in length to support a tarp roof. If you're building in a wooded area, find trees hung together with their bases touching each other (known as "mutual support") and choose the tallest member of the group.

Step 6: Spread out some tarp on the ground for cover, and then tie it tightly at both ends and sides using rope or twine. Begin with a large tarp of at least 8 feet by 10 feet.

Use brown canvas tarps because they are heavy-duty, waterproof, and won't rot in the elements.

Step 7: Spread the tarp out directly in front of one end of the ridge pole and then place some small twigs or branches across it to hold it down. These will become your floorboards. The floor should be at least 6 inches above the ground so that water and leaves don't come up under it.

If you're building your shelter on hard ground, you can use two small logs to create a frame for your floorboards that keep them spaced apart for a little extra insulation.

Step 8: If you're building on a particular ground like beaches or rock cliffs, you can make a "rock wall" using some rocks and branches from the forest floor and tying them in an "L" shape between two trees. Then you can use twine or rope hanging from the walls to hang up your clothes.

Step 9: Use some long branches or longer sticks to prop up two corners of the tarp roof. Then crawl into your shelter and use a knife (or another cutting tool) to cut one end of the tarp off so that it hangs down about 6-12 inches below your floorboards (to increase insulation).

You'll want to make your lean-to about 4 feet high at its peak for maximum headroom and good ventilation.

Step 10: Tie more long branches together to create the rafters for your tarp roof. Then use rope or twine and tie them to the underside of your ridge pole and another large rigid beam. These will keep your tarp from sagging downwards in areas where people are standing or sitting, so they should be placed evenly across the entire shelter.

If you don't have flexible tree trunks (or large flexible branches) as support beams, then you can use thick tree limbs that are about 2 inches in diameter or more significant as "false" rafters instead.

Step 11: Once your tarp roof is in place, start tying the ridge pole to the arch tree at both ends. Then crawl under it and connect it all the way across so all four sides support it.

If you want to make a permanent shelter from thick tree trunks or branches, then leave just one end of a chapter sticking out above your roofing material for ventilation.

Step 12: Add more branches across your ridge pole and other roof beams for insulation and ventilation purposes. Also, add some tarp over the top of your floorboards to keep out rain, snow, and leaves.

If you want to make your shelter more durable, you can dig a trench around it and line it with stones before putting all of your floorboards in. This will keep the floorboards from rotting or drying out.

Step 13: Add some more layers of the tarp, branches, and twine to your roofing material for extra insulation. Then tie the ends of each layer together so that there are no gaps for rain and snow to enter.

You want your shelter's roof to be as strong as possible because it will bear most of the weight absorbed by all those tarp layers across its surface area.

Step 14: Once your roof is in place, add some more branches to the top of your rafters for extra insulation. You'll notice that these stay close to the underside of your tarp roof and don't protrude upwards too much.

You want to tie each layer of tarp across your roofing material because it will help hold the layers in place and prevent them from shifting or moving around.

Step 15: Add an extra tarp on top of your rafters for much-needed insulation. Then tie these sheets together to keep the rain (and snow) from entering through any gaps or holes.

You can make your shelter more durable by lining the inside of your roof with branches and rocks for extra insulation.

If you built a traditional lean-to shelter or an A-frame tent, then all that's left is to create a fire and call it a night!

Or if you built any of the other shelters, get a fire going and snuggle up inside for the night.

Types of Shelters You Can Make in Case of a Disaster, Emergency, or Attack

We will break down the most common types of shelters people can construct in case of a disaster or emergency, so you'll know which is best for you.

Underground Shelter:

But if it's safety that matters most to you, then this type of shelter might be what gets your stamp of approval. With these types of shelters, you can stay underground for weeks at a time without ever having to worry about fresh air.

For these underground shelters, you'll need:

1) A hole dug into the ground. You can use a shovel, backhoe, pickaxe, or entrenching tool. Keep in mind that your shelter is going to be underground. That means no windows and just enough room to wiggle around. Since these are holes dug into the ground (so they're "underground"), you'll want to make sure it's secure before letting family members or pets inside.

2) Duct tape. A railroad tie will also work, but some duct tape works as well since it's easier to take apart and put together as needed.

3) A few blankets for warmth.

4) Some nonperishable food.

5) One extra change of clothes and at least one pairs of shoes each for each member of your family.

6) Your favorite photo or memorabilia you'd like to keep in the shelter.

Tunnel Shelter:

Tunnels are great for this, and they're pretty easy to build with just some woods, plastic sheeting (or some other waterproof material), and a tarp.

For these tunnels, you'll need:

1) Large pieces of plywood that are at least 4 feet wide by 8 feet long. The type of plywood depends on where you live, so it might be best to get the opinion of your local home improvement store. These can be pre-cut, or you can make them yourself.

2) A tape measure or a ruler.

3) A hand saw if you have one.

4) Some plastic sheeting.

5) A tarp or something similar to help cover the tunnel entrance but still allows in some light.

Home Shelter:

This type of shelter is excellent because it can be built in almost any space you have at your home. These shelters are great for prepping for natural disasters or even as a listening post where you can monitor the outside world.

For these home shelters, you'll need:

1) A safe space to place a radio, television, and alarm system. This could include an attic, basement, garage, or even a window that allows light and airflow. Ensure that the radios or TVs don't get too hot (like an outdoor antenna) with fire threats (like lightning). Also, consider having extra batteries for radios and TVs if they're something like outdoor antennas.

2) Some wood or other support materials.

3) A windbreak is a roof that can withstand high winds or protect your home during the rain (like plywood).

4) an ample open space with plenty of electrical outlets for electricity. You can put it in an extension cord and run it up through the ceiling, where it is plugged into a switched outlet. Or you can have generators that run off natural gas, propane, or solar power.

Community Shelter:

If you'd like to do something for the community and want to make sure that others are safe, then a community shelter might just be what you're looking for. This type of shelter is excellent because it provides shelter and a sense of community that can keep spirits up during a disaster.

For these community shelters, you'll need:

1) A large building or area to use as a shelter. This could include houses, fire stations, schools, churches, synagogues, or other large, sturdy structures where people can take refuge. If it's a school or other public place, be sure to get permission from the local government before working on the structure.

2) A water supply from natural sources or a small well that can provide water to everyone.

3) Some food for everyone, especially if you're acting as the primary food source.

GETTING FOOD
AND STORING IT

CHAPTER 4

TRAVEL NOTES

Fishing, Hunting, and Trapping

Fishing

Whether you are enjoying a trip into the wilderness or find yourself in a survival situation, bodies of water, rivers, and streams are a rich source of water and food. Learning how to fish with the bare basics can be a fun experiment to enjoy with friends and family or it could save your life.

You can purchase a very basic fishing kit, containing a simple hook and some line, to keep in your backpack or you can make your own with what you can find around you.

Fishing Hooks

If you don't have a fishing hook, or perhaps you lost the one you had to a particularly feisty fish, you can use things you may have with you or natural materials to create rudimentary but effective fishing hooks.

Fishing Line

If you are out of proper fishing line, cut a length of paracord and remove the inner strands from the outer casing. Use the inner strands as a fishing line. If you have dental floss with you, this will also work as a fishing line. If you don't have dental floss or paracord to spare, you can make use of the intestinal lining of animals for a successful hunt.

Bait

Casting your hook and line is useless without the right bait. Expert fishermen will extol the virtues of knowing exactly what kind of bait is best suited for what species of fish. This does have its merits as certain types of fish are attracted to certain types of foods. However, when you're living off the land or find yourself fishing for survival, you may not be able to lay your hands on a particular fish's ideal snack.

Hunting

As far as the small and medium game is considered, shotguns are the most versatile and best-suited weapons. There are many different choices available in the market that have pros and cons.

Hunting: Why?

In survival situations, we are forced to face extreme conditions. In such conditions, we need an ample amount of proteins and calories. While these can be consumed in the form of plants, if you want quicker and much denser sources of proteins, the best option for you is consuming animals. Survival hunting is an essential skill that you need to learn. Survival situations need a lot of energy that can be easily gained from animals. Edible animals provide concentrated calories; that is why survival hunting can make a huge difference in situations of crisis.

In the wilderness, the most accessible and practical wild animals are small game, reptiles, fish, invertebrates, and amphibians. Certain invertebrates like mollusks have already been covered in a previous chapter. All the above-stated animals make the highest amount of sense in a survival-hunting situation. These animals are small, and you can collect a bunch of them with ease. They need little to no weapons; in fact, you can gather many of these with your bare hands.

Hunting Safety Tips to Remember

Here is a shortlist of tips that you should remember to keep yourself safe and secure while hunting. Hunters are provided with a lot of safety tips and tricks. Most beginners tend to remember these religiously; however, with time, people tend to become complacent. When this happens, the risk of getting into an accident increases manifold. Remember, safety should always be your number one priority. Take some time and review all the lessons given below and pass them on to other hunters to keep them safe as well.

- Always treat a firearm as if it is loaded even if it is not. Never climb a tree or a ladder with a loaded rifle.

- Always be certain of your target and identify it clearly. You should also check what is behind your target as a powerful projectile often travels for a long distance.

- Before daylight or after dark, always use a flashlight while passing around another hunter's area. This will let the hunter know your whereabouts, and it will also help you to prevent any mishaps.

- Always check your rifle multiple times and make sure that it is unloaded.

- Let your friends and family know about where you are going. Many times hunters get into accidents, but no one can find them because no one knows about their location. Hunters tend to be secretive, but it is recommended to let at least a few people known about your location.

- Always use a harness while hunting from an elevated stand, like a tree stand.

- Always wear hunter orange vest whenever it is necessary. You can never know who else is in the area.

- A lot of accidents related to firearms happen at the truck, especially while loading and unloading them. Beware and use extra caution.

- When hunting, deer never wear any white clothing. You may get mistaken for a deer.

Remember, accidents are highly common, especially in the outdoors and wilderness, but with some care and vigilance, you can avoid them with ease. Just remember that safety should always be your first priority.

Trapping

If you plant to catch food in the wilderness, you need to have a good and working knowledge of traps that can be used to catch three kinds of animals- fish, mammals, and fowl.

If you are caught in the wilderness for a long time, always remember that living food never spoils. So instead of hunting or gathering a lot of food at one time and trying to preserve it, it is better to gather and hunt it fresh. This can prove to be a great asset in hot weather; however, it can make things difficult if you are caught in an area with large predatory animals. In such cases, you need to make decisions quickly.

Trapping is great for animals such as frogs and turtles that can be stored in a bag or a sack for a long time.

Traps are subjective to methods, animals, and seasons. For instance, certain traps can be used in certain seasons only to trap certain species. Traps are indiscriminate, which means that you cannot control the type or species of animal you catch; however, you can still have some control over the trap by adjusting the size and bait. This will bring down the risk of catching a non-target or undesirable animal.

Bait Animals

You can find good meat sources around the edge of water resources. Remember that meat is meat, and it does not always have to come from furry mammals. In fact, a great and easy to procure a source of meat is fish and other aquatic animals. Crayfish, frogs, turtles, and fish all are sources of meat that can be consumed and used as baits.

It is recommended to catch food items for yourself and then use the leftovers as a bait to trap bigger prey. If you are ever caught in an area where there is no water source nearby, you can still trap small mammals such as rats, mice, and chipmunks, which can be used for similar results. It is recommended to combine both methods to get better results in the end. Some of these can even become a full-fledged meal if you manage to catch turtles and large fish.

Your first priority should always be catching animals that rank low on the food chain. It does not matter if you do not plan to consume them; you can always use them as baits. A baited trap is more likely to yield you better results than a non-baited one. You can then work your way up the food chain, and if you continue to persevere, you will find better and more fulfilling food in no time.

How to make them

Making your own traps are better than buying them from a store. They will be more effective, cheaper and easier to make.

Turtle Trap

Turtles can be easily trapped in meat or fish. You will only need a sturdy box trap with two compartments separated by a stiff divider: one for the bait and the other to catch the turtle. The bait should include eggs, fish, and greasy food like bacon. Make sure the trap is predator proof and securely fastened. Stake out the area for a few days to see if any turtle will come by.

Snares

A snare is used to trap animals using their legs and feet. It is used in a variety of ways, but mostly as a means to make small catches from the ground into larger ones by making them hop towards the hunter or towards the cage containing them. The method consists of placing a flexible noose around the animal's neck, fastening it to something else, and then to a stake in the ground. Snaring can be used effectively on many different small animals. The noose can be made from any material that is stiff enough and long enough to wrap itself around an animal's neck.

Bait traps

A live bait trap is made by setting up an elaborate cage or pen near a place where animals such as raccoons or turkeys are known to frequent. The trap is made of thin wire mesh that allows the animal to see, smell, and get the bait inside. The animal will try to reach into the cage through the mesh, and it either can't get out or will be too afraid to try. You will also need to make sure that no predators like dogs or cats are around. Another type of bait trap is a deadfall trap, where a heavy object such as a rock, log, or anvil falls on an animal when it steps on a trigger in its path.

Storing and Preservation

In difficult and survival-related situations, it is necessary to learn how to store food. In difficult situations and crises, you will often be faced with lean times when you will have nothing to eat. In such cases, if you preserve your food, you will never have to go hungry. Preserving food is quite simple.

- Meat: Make jerky by salting and drying it.

- Tubers and Roots: These can be dried well and then stored in a dry and cool place.

Preserving Meat

The most common and easy way of preserving meat is by cutting it in thin strips.

The strips should just be an inch wide and try to keep under a quarter-inch thick.

You make the strips as long as possible. You can also make them as long as per your needs and requirements. Remove as much fat as you can.

Hang the ribbon on a drying rack or a similar place where they will be exposed to sunlight directly.

Let the strips cure until they start to crack if folded.

You can store this jerky in a cool and non-humid area, such as the back of a cave. You can also store these jerkies in a dry hole in the ground. Just line the hole with some dry grass and cover it with a flat rock after storing the jerky.

Small Animals

You can store small animals by drying them.

You can use this method to store chipmunks, squirrels, and certain birds.

Just skin, clean, and open the dead animals and put them in the sun to let them dry and dehydrate in the sun.

Once the meat is dry enough, pound the meat with a rock. This will break the bones and bring out the marrow.

Let the meat dry once again. This will cure the marrow. If you skip this step, the marrow will spoil the meat.

Roots and Tubers

You can store tubers and roots by drying them.

Clean the roots and tubers that you plan to store.

Make thin slices of these tubers and roots and let them dry completely on a flat rock under sunlight.

Leafy Vegetables

You can store leafy vegetables and herbs by bundling them and hanging them upside down from a shady and dry place. You can preserve them inside your hut or makeshift shelter.

Practice!

Always practice foraging, cooking, and all other skills before you plant to use them in real survival situations. When you are forced to face the real deal, you will be scared and nervous. This is not the time to learn and practice new skills.

Living and surviving in the wilderness is a hard-earned knowledge the needs a lot of practice and skills. Even if you never get lost in the wilderness, you still need to learn how to survive in it to avoid any risks.

Warning

Remember, never consume any wild food, whether plant or animal, without being completely sure about its identity. Use a field guide and, if possible, try to learn under an expert hunter and forager to sharpen your skills of identification

GROW WHAT
AND WHEN

CHAPTER 5

TRAVEL NOTES

a. *Allium carolinianum*   b. *Angelica glauca*   c. *Arisaema jacquemontii*   d. *Berberis chitria*

e. *Heracleum pinnatum*   f. *Bistorta affinis*   g. *Castanea sativa*   h. *Diplazium esculentum*

i. *Equisetum arvense*   j. *Oxyria digyna*   k. *Bergenia stracheyi*   l. *Hippophae rhamnoides*

m. Local folk eating *Rheum australe*   n. *Malus baccata*   o. *Morchella esculenta*   p. *Pinus gerardiana*

q. *Sinopodophyllum hexandrum*   r. *Prunus mira*   s. *Sorbus lanata*   t. *Pyrus pashia*

u. *Rhododendron arboreum*   v. *Rosa webbiana*   w. *Sparassis crispa*   x. *Taxus wallichiana*

Common Edible Plants

Many plants that grow in our front and backyard are edible. These include dandelion, clover, burdock, plantain, and violets that are edible and are often found in rural areas. Along with these usual suspects, there are many other varieties of wild but edible plants that can be used as sustenance in the wilderness. It is recommended to get a proper foraging guide to learn more about these plants. Many wild plants look like other edible plants but are extremely toxic. To avoid any risk, a proper foraging guide is necessary.

The case becomes even more difficult in the case of fungi. Edible fungi are full of essential nutrients, but there are multitudes of fungi that are poisonous and can be life-threatening. Unless you are an expert forager, it is recommended to avoid wild fungi altogether.

To be able to forage for your dinner means you should ideally have in-depth knowledge about the plants that are available in your area (or the particular patch of the wilderness). You need to know what you can eat and what cannot.

Grass

Grass that is young, tender, and has whitish tips is generally edible and tastes okay. It can be consumed raw.

Roots and Tubers

Tubers and roots grow underneath the soil. They are highly nutritious but often require cooking. Yams, potatoes, onions, etc. are all different forms of tubers or roots.

Seeds and Nuts

Nuts and seeds of a variety of plants are not only edible, but they are full of nutrients as well. Any seed that tastes acidic or bitter is generally not safe for eating. In most of the cases, a seed or nut can be made edible by either boiling them or soaking them in water overnight.

Leaves

It is possible to consume the leaves of a variety of plants raw or by cooking them. Nettles, watercress, spinach, etc. all can be eaten in the wilderness. Leaves that have a strong bitter taste can be toxic and should be avoided.

Fruit & Berries

Fruits and berries are commonly available in the supermarket, but the fruits that we see, such as pears, apples, and bananas, etc. are all a result of thousands of years of selective cultivation. This means many fruits and berries that appear in the wild may not have the same tastes as the ones available in the market. Similarly, a lot of fruits and berries available in the wild can be harmful if consumed. Do not consume fruit if you are not aware of its origin. Avoid eating white berries, as they are most likely to be toxic.

Things to Avoid

An expert bushcrafter knows what to eat and what not to eat. Here is a short list of rules that you should keep in mind while eating out in the wilderness.

Almond-Like Taste

If a plant tastes like almonds, it probably contains prussic acid. This acid is toxic to humans. In many cases, this acid can be taken care of by boiling the plant. If the plant loses its almond-like taste after boiling or soaking, it is generally safe to eat. Do throw the water away immediately.

Smell

If a fruit or plant has an off-putting smell, it is better to avoid it. The human nose or the sense of smell is a result of prolonged evolution. It has evolved in such a way that it can warn us against dangerous foods. It is better to avoid foods that smell bad. (Exceptions include durian etc.)

Red Shades

It is recommended to avoid the color red, as the plant is most likely to be toxic or dangerous to us. There are many exceptions to this rule, for instance, apples, tomatoes, strawberries, etc. but if you are not sure whether a red plant, a berry, or a fruit are absolutely safe for consumption, it is better to avoid them.

Bitterness or Acidity

Any plant that tastes extremely hot or bitter should be avoided, as it will generally make you sick. It can even prove to be a threat to your life.

Fungi

Fungi are full of nutrients, and they taste delicious, but these factors come at a huge cost. A lot of fungi are toxic, and a lot of fungi look alike. It is quite difficult to discern the toxic varieties from the edible one. If you are a beginner, it is better to avoid fungi altogether.

Uncertainty

If you are uncertain about something, whether it is edible or not, the best thing to do is to avoid it altogether. If avoiding it is not an option, taste a small bite of the object, but DO NOT swallow it. If the sample tastes good i.e., not too bitter or acidic, then swallow a little bit and wait. If you do not see any negative reactions within an hour, the plant is usually safe for consumption. This should be a last resort tactic only. If possible, avoid anything that you do not recognize.

Boiling or cooking can generally reduce certain toxins and bitterness from the plant. It is still recommended to study the local plants carefully before making any decisions.

Choosing the Right Plants

The best way to check whether a plant is fit for consumption or not is by utilizing the ITEM method. ITEM stands for:

Identification

Identify the plant by referring to a multitude of sources. It is quite easy to misidentify a plant. Consuming a misidentified plant can make you severely ill or may even lead to death.

Time of Year

Always check the time or period of growth/blooming of a plant by referring to a foraging guide. If you find a plant growing out of season, it is most likely to be a different plant that you have misidentified. It is better to avoid out-of-season plants

93

altogether.

Environment

Like growth time, season, and period, it is recommended to check whether the plant is growing in its proper habitat and appropriate atmosphere or not. For instance, if you find a plant that generally grows in marshy lands growing in a dry spot, it is more likely to be a different plant that you have misidentified.

Methods

The last item in the ITEM technique is 'method.' In this technique, you need to learn how to harvest and prepare a food item before you consume it. This is necessary as, in the case of certain plants, the stem is not edible, but the leaves are. The vice versa is true too. In some cases, the foliage is edible, but the berries aren't. Some plants can be consumed raw, while others need to be cooked before eating. It is recommended to follow a foraging guide to learn a variety of facts about many different plants. If possible, try to learn the nuances regarding foraging from an expert.

Wild Edibles

Here are some simple plants that are commonly available around you. You can find some more information regarding these and some other plants in the next chapter.

Cattails

Cattails are not only edible and delicious, but they are also full of medicinal properties. The shoots can be eaten raw or boiled. The rootstock and tubers are edible as well. The seed and the pollen collected from the seed can be used as flour. The tender seed heads can be enjoyed like corn on the cob.

Field Parsnip

Field parsnip was a highly popular food item for a long time; however, it has fallen out of use in recent times. The root of the plant contains a lot of starch and can be baked or cooked like a potato.

Note: Handle this plant with care as mishandling may lead to contact dermatitis.

Dandelion

Dandelion is edible, delicious, and has a lot of medicinal properties. They are often used in salads and can be eaten out of hand too. They contain high amounts of vitamin A. Its roots can be dried, ground, and used as a coffee substitute.

Burdock

Young leaves of the burdock plant are especially good for salad greens, and the large taproot is fine starch.

Burdock (Edible)

Burdock is also known as an arrowhead. It is an edible water plant that has edible tubers that contain high amounts of starch.

Leeks and Ramps

Many different plants have edible bulbs, including leeks, onion, and garlic. Bulbs can be stored for a long time in a dry and cool place. They can last for the whole season. They are delicious and can add a great taste to otherwise bland food.

Bushcraft Tip

While charcoal is not a plant, it is recommended to carry it all the time while foraging. It is a crucial resource that can save your life in the case of accidental plant or food poisoning. Just grind some charcoal, mix it water, and drink it. This solution will induce vomiting instantly. Charcoal is highly absorbent, and it will soak up a lot of toxins to prevent further damage.

Outdoor Cooking, Safety and Ethic

Making Utensils

One of the most important tools that nature has blessed human beings with is fire. It can really make or break your chances of survival in difficult situations. Fire does not only provide you warm, heat, and light, it can also be used to form, cut, bend, and create implements. The heat generated by a fire can be used to cook things. In exceptionally difficult times, fire can make things a bit easy for you. You can make even utensils using a fire.

It is possible to make simple utensils and cooking containers with the help of fire. This includes everything from a cup, pot, spoons, etc. All of these can be made in the wilderness. Just look for a good branch or suitable log. Try to find a piece of wood that is neither rotten nor punky. It should be big enough to fashion a practical utensil or container. A piece of wood that can hold a couple of quart of liquids and solids will make a brilliant utensil and can be used to cook a variety of dishes too.

There are many trees in the forest, and some of them can be potentially poisonous, avoid these. Generally, it is recommended to stick to hemlocks, pines, cedars, hickories, firs, and sassafras to make cooking utensils as well as containers. Hardwood trees are much better than softwoods as they take more time to burn, but they can also hold foodstuff for a long time by preventing the liquids from seeping into the walls of the containers.

Once you have found a good-sized and high-quality chunk of wood, chip away the bark from one side until you end up with a flat side, now pick some embers from your bone fire and put them in the center of the chunk of wood and let the embers burn slowly into the wood.

Coals generally burn down directly, and this will help you to create a natural bowl shape. This technique can be used to fashion bowls and containers of various sizes. You can make a bowl large enough to hold a couple of quart of liquids in one hour using this method. For hardwoods such as oak, the process may take longer. You just need to have some patience and practice to make different sized containers. With dedication, you will be able to make a proper set of utensils in no time.

Once you have burned off depression as per your need, you need to trim out the flaky and burnt residue. This can be done using a stone. Once you have scraped out these details, sand it using a round stone until it looks ready. This vessel will be highly effective for cooking as well as storing food.

You can use the same method to fashion a spoon. To do so, just take 5-7 inch long and ½ inch thick piece of wood and put a lump of single hot coal on one end of the piece. Blow the ember frequently until a small, hollow depression is formed. Scrape out the burnt and flaky area and carve the rest using a sharp rock. You can also give the rock your desired shape using this rock.

Stones can be used for a lot more than just carving and scraping the utensils. Stones can be used as all-purpose tools, and every survivalist must learn how to use them efficiently. A simple rock can do almost all the things that a knife, an ax, or a piece of sandpaper can do. Mother nature has provided us with different kinds, textures, and shapes of rocks to choose from. Use them wisely for a variety of purposes.

Rocks can be used to form rudimentary knives. To do so, just struck two rocks together until a sharp edge is formed. This sharpened rock can then be used to cut and scrape things. You can also use rocks for whetting and grinding. It is also possible to create a 'dish' using rocks that can be used to grind grains. To shape a rock into a dish, hit a rock with another harder rock. Carefully shape the rock in circular and pecking motions. This process will take a long time, but ultimately you will be able to create a good and long-lasting utensil. Any tool that can enhance your chance of survival is a great tool; it does not matter if it takes a long time to do so.

Along with rocks, you can also use bones to make good and efficient tools. Choose and use suitable bones and sharpen them with a rock. You can make simple but serviceable scraper, knives, and awls using bones.

Cooking Techniques

All the animals that you plan to eat should always be cleaned and cooked thoroughly; otherwise, the parasites infesting the animals may make your severely ill.

All creatures (except insects) should be skinned, eviscerated, and checked carefully for any signs of abnormalities and diseases. Do not throw away the 'bad' specimens; you can use them as a bait. Certain plants need to be cooked before they can be edible. Cooking produces heat, and heat destroys a lot of toxins present in plants.

Here is a list of various food preparation methods that can be used in the wilderness.

Rock Boiling

This one of the oldest methods of cooking, and it is also one of the most useful forms, especially in situations where you are forced to cook using a container that cannot be placed directly on the fire. You can use heated rocks for cooking food in hollow wooden utensils. This method is also useful if you want to conserve and retain the nutrition present in ingredients.

It is recommended to use round and small rocks in this method. They should ideally be the size of golf balls. Avoid taking rocks from damp areas or from water bodies, as rocks tend to have tiny cracks that may harbor parasites and other microbes. The cracks can prove to be dangerous in other ways too. For instance, when you heat rocks, it can vaporize the water present in the cracks that may lead to the explosion of the stone. This is why it is recommended to use on bone-dry rocks. Avoid quartz, flint, sandstone, obsidian, and any other hard rocks that form with the help of silicate. These tend to shatter when heated and can ruin your meal.

To cook your meal, you will need at least six to ten small stones. Heat these stones in the fire for at least a couple of hours.

Put the animal parts and plant that you want to cook in your wooden utensil and cover them with water. Then using a set of tongs or two sticks, carefully pick up a stone and drop it in the utensil carefully. The water around the rock will start to boil at once. Continue to add rocks at regular intervals until the complete liquid starts to bubble. When the bubbling starts to slow down, remove the rocks one by one and replace them with new rocks. Repeat this process until your food is evenly cooked.

Spit Cooking

This is another ancient method of cooking which was used by our ancestors. This method is quicker as compared to other methods, but it destroys a lot of nutritional value from the food. In this method, an animal is skinned, gutted, and cleaned and is then skewered and roasted on an open fire. The skewers should be made with non-toxic wood. Suspend the skewers over the heat and turn them around frequently. It is better to cook the meat over coal as an open flame may char the skewers and the meat. You can also roast the various tubers and roots in the spit and make rudimentary 'shish kebobs.' Wrap the meat and roots in non-toxic and edible leaves and roast them directly in the coals.

Pit Cooking

This is an effective method that can also safeguard nutrition; the only problem with this type of cooking is that it takes more effort and time.

To do this, dig a hole in the ground according to the size of the animal you plan to cook.

Line the bottom of the hole with dry and flat rocks and build a fire over these rocks.

Let the fire burn for at least three hours or until the rocks start to glow due to heat. Remove the coals and scrape the place clean.

Add a layer of green grass over the rocks. The grass should be non-poisonous, and the layer should be at least eight inches thick.

On top of the layer of grass, but the food that you plan to cook. This may include roots, meat, tubers, rhizomes, and any other hearty foods. Do not put herbs and leafy vegetables, as they will burn away in this form of cooking.

Now put a layer of green grass over the food. Again the grass should be non-poisonous, and the layer should be at least eight inches thick.

Seal the pit with various slabs of bark.

Cover the pit with a six-inch layer of earth and let the food cook for at least 2-3 hours.

Once done, carefully scrape the dirt away, remove the bark and pull out the greenery. The grass will be steamy and hot. This method will not only cook your food properly, but it will also retain all the nutrients and natural juices of the food.

Fry-Rock Method

In this method, flat and thin rock is cleaned of all debris and dirt. You can clean the rock with dried grasses and horsetail to make it extra clean.

Prop the rock carefully with the help of three or more small stones. Put it over the fire and let the rock get hot.

Once the rock is hot enough, you can use it as a metal frying pan.

Frying destroys a lot of nutrients, so be quick.

Rock Oven Baking

You can make a rudimentary over just next to your fire pit. Construct a rectangular structure with rocks and keep the opening towards the fire.

Close off all the sides, back, and top with sod and dirt. This box will catch and retain the heat produced by the fire. It will allow you to bake your food just like a regular oven.

To control the temperature, just move the fire around or let it die if you want to reduce it.

When removing food from the over, keep your hands away from the rocks as they will be extremely hot and may cause severe injuries.

Board or Rock Reflector System

In this method, you need a rock or a flat piece of wood from a non-poisonous tree.

Put the tree at an angle of 45 degrees so that the heat from the bonfire will slowly cook your food placed against the slab.

Turn the food frequently to ensure proper cooking.

Tools

Cooking requires equipment—everything from knives to cut meat to pots to cook it in to plates to serve it on. But to carry all that equipment would take up a lot of room and a lot of weight. In this chapter, we'll talk about what equipment you really need, how you can lighten your load, and what tools and utensils you can actually make from materials in your environment.

Almost any tool you could possibly need for processing and cooking food can be made from the landscape in a pinch for sure. However, the most difficult to make—especially depending on local resources and skill level—are cutting tools and containers. Peripheral items, from cutting boards to spoons and spatulas, are easy enough to improvise if you need to.

Cooking Equipment Materials

Before we get into actually choosing and using containers, we should discuss material types a bit to have a better understanding of the pros and cons depending on the situation and the way we are using it. Obviously we can fashion utensils from natural materials and improvise cookware from cans, which we'll describe later in this chapter. But for this discussion, let's start off with talking of dedicated containers we may carry for cooking that are bought new or used and the types of materials they are made from.

We will not speak to cooking with tin and copper in this book although for re-enactment purposes they are a viable option. However, brass buckets make a good addition if you can't afford the heavy stainless steel kind. Brass buckets can often be found at estate sales and antique malls at reasonable prices.

Cast Iron

The biggest advantage to cast iron is even heating. It takes time to heat this material but it retains heat well and cooks food evenly due to this property. Cold spots caused by a sudden change in wind direction will be rare if ever. Lots of great cookware is made from cast iron, from ovens to pans, griddles, and biscuit and bread pans.

One of things most often carried in westward expansion where wagons were available was the family's cast iron, especially the Dutch oven. Because these come in many sizes from 1 quart to as large as 14" across, they can be fitted well to your needs and form of conveyances.

The biggest downside from a traveling standpoint is weight. Cast iron also requires a certain amount of care for it to maintain its seasoning and keep food from sticking.

Sheet Steel

Sheet steel, both thick and thin, has been used for making cookware since as long as it has been available. Steel is generally lighter than cast iron but still heavy unless the gauge is thin. Many nice old cold-handle skillets are available; they make great camp cooking tools that weigh very little compared to cast iron and will season much like cast iron, since they're made of a porous metal. Rust is the main enemy of this material (much like cast iron) so some care must be taken to maintain it.

Enamelware

Enameled cookware came to the U.S. around 1850. Americans began to own enamel-lined culinary utensils, but they were very plain—nothing like the colourful mottled surfaces that were yet to come. The Stuart & Peterson foundry in Philadelphia was making enamel-lined cast-iron pots in the 1860s.

Enamelware is an iconic part of camp cooking, and it is still as viable an option today as it was in the late nineteenth and early twentieth centuries. It is lightweight, easy to clean, transfers heat well, and has few drawbacks. The main issue is the chipping that occurs from abuse. But drinking vessels from this material are hard to beat for a good cup of morning coffee. It can be found in good condition, is cheap enough, and will last a lifetime if cared for.

Stainless Steel

An improvement over carbon steel in both strength and rust resistance, stainless is by far one of my personal favorites for camp cookware. It will never cook as well as cast iron in my opinion, but the tradeoff in terms of weight and maintenance alone gives it high marks for use over time and seasons.

It transfers heat fairly well, although not as well as cast iron. Stainless steel is getting less and less expensive, so it is generally very affordable. There are very fancy pieces on the market that combine stainless steel with copper or aluminum bottoms for better heat transfer but these are not necessary for simple camp meals.

Aluminum

Let me first say that until I see conclusive research that cooking in aluminum has major issues on health I will continue to use it. However, each person should make his or her own judgments about this material. It has so many advantages from a weight and cost standpoint it is hard to ignore.

Aluminum has fantastic conductivity and is very durable and lightweight. Modern anodized aluminum takes away the concerns of health risks, is inexpensive to buy, and gives a helpful nonstick surface to cook on as well. The only issue is from scratching, as with most other nonstick coatings.

There are even Dutch ovens made from aluminum that are a third the weight of cast iron. Aluminum transfers heat very well, so coffee cups of this material make drinking hot coffee a dangerous game.

Titanium

Titanium is the latest and greatest material for camp cookware, but is it the best? In my opinion this fantastic metal, used for making the lightest of modern cookware, is a great resource. If you are counting every ounce in the pack, that is where the advantages begin and end for me. The drawbacks are that titanium is very expensive, tends to warp in the direct heat of a campfire, and it does not cook evenly at all. Like aluminum, it's a good heat conductor so it heats too fast and cools too fast for cooking.

WATER COLLECTION
AND TREATMENT

CHAPTER 6

One of those things is about sourcing fresh water. You can always be sure of finding drinking water by looking for precipitation sources such as rivers, streams, and lakesides. You can also look for water sources by looking out for plants that are growing nearby. When plants grow, they absorb water from the soil and transpire it through their leaves. Water vapor will escape to the atmosphere through the stomata of the plants' leaves. Water will condense on cool surfaces such as rocks or tree branches, which will later drip down into collection puddles. The problem is that there might not always be a suitable collection source nearby. And if you're way off the beaten path, you might not find any source at all. There is another way to get water, however, and it's the only reliable method for getting fresh water in the wilderness. This method would be known as water sourcing and purification. Water sourcing is the art of finding an adequate source of water for yourself. Purifying means to remove impurities from fresh water so that you could drink it without any health concerns. The two processes involve a little bit of back science and science-y knowledge about what life forms live where in a given ecosystem.

Water Sourcing

Water Sourcing can be done in different ways—the best way being to follow what the plants around you do. Plants capture water from the atmosphere and transpire through their leaves, which will later drip down into collection puddles and soak into the soil. If fresh water is available in an area, it will be easy to find out because the environment there would be teeming with vegetation and other life forms. You can then look for areas that seem to have a surplus of flora, such as drier areas that don't get much precipitation. It will take skill and practice to determine which sources are reliable (those close by) and which ones aren't (those far away). This process requires you to study your subject thoroughly or learn about them through your research. You can also use a map or find a guidebook for where you want to go. With the map, you can get an idea of where to find sources, which are more reliable than others.

Lakes and ponds in mountain ranges and in areas near them in dry regions. Rivers in sparsely populated areas or in redwood forests. Lakes with consistent water levels. Water Sourcing is only the first step in water sourcing and purification! It's not enough to just find a source, you need to see if it's safe for consumption. Water sourcing is easy; water purification is another story.

Water Purification

Once you find a potential source of fresh water, you still have to check it in order to make sure that there are no harmful organisms and pathogens present in it. Before you drink from a source of water, it's important to analyze its chemical composition or pH level. You can do this by first testing the pH level on a scale of 1-14 with a device such as a pH meter. If you can't buy one right away, you can use baking soda instead of a meter—a pinch of soda mixed with a short amount of water will give you an approximate reading on the pH level. You can test the food value as well as the biological value by mixing some into aquariums. Then wait for some time for those to come up from the bottom and see if there are any problems. If it passes both your tests, you can start drinking the water by boiling it first. If the water comes from a small pond or lake, you can do all of this right away. You can also start filtering out potential pollutants by using a drinking straw. The drinking straw will filter out impurities like leaves and fill up with impure water. When there is enough impure water accumulated, you can tilt the straw to the side and let the impure water leak out into a container or on to the ground. If that doesn't work, you can use other filtering systems such as some sort of cloth lined with activated charcoal (for instance, linen), which will sift out contaminants.

Filtering water is not always necessary when sourcing water in the wilderness, but it's up to you whether you want to spend some extra time filtering it or not. Lastly, you can also use a technique called "squeezing" if the whole system is working properly. Squeezing involves squeezing out all of the water from a container, which will make the remaining water purer. You can squeeze by using your hands or using some sort of tool such as a ball bearing with rounded edges. When you have enough purified drinking water, it's time to return to our starting point. Water purification is an important skill that every wilderness traveler should have. You can always look up a guidebook or a map for where you want to go to get the best water sources. And if you're planning your trip, make sure that water purification is top priority!

5 Ways to Purify Water in the Wilderness

In the event of a natural disaster, being able to safely drink water is a top priority. However, when you're in the wilderness and the only water source you have access to is contaminated, there are a few simple techniques that can be used to purify it.

Find out what these five methods are below!

1) Boiling - Boil for at least 5 minutes or bring water to a boil and let it cool before drinking. This will kill any microorganisms in the water that can make people sick. This method is effective against bacteria and protozoa but not viruses.

2) Chlorine Water Treatment - Always drink from a clean water source that has been treated with at least 25 drops of household chlorine bleach such as Clorox. This will kill 99% of bacteria and viruses. Chlorine is an oxidizer and works by adding free radicals to cells, killing them. A bleach chemical reaction occurs when the chlorine comes in contact with the contaminants, killing the bacteria and viruses.

3) UV Water Treatment - Light can help destroy microorganisms and parasites in water by destroying their DNA and RNA respectively. Buy a SteriPEN or pick up a Steripen Pencil for really long trips. Just hold the pen in the water for 60 seconds while it purifies the water.

4) Iodine Water Treatment - Use at least 15 drops of 2% iodine per liter, mix well and allow to stand for 30 minutes. Iodine is effective against bacteria but not viruses.

5) Ultraviolet Light Purification - A great way to purify water is by using a UV wand that hangs off your backpack or tactical pack. These are lightweight, portable and run on batteries. They can also be used to purify water when you don't have any other options available; they will kill 99% of most microbes in the water. Just hold the wand in the water for 60 seconds while it purifies the water.

LIGHT
A FIRE

CHAPTER 7

TRAVEL NOTES

How to Build the Perfect fire?

How to Build fire for Cooking?

The purpose is to convert all wood to coal at the same time. This can produce uniform flame, not burning flame or burning black cookware. It can also get the longest cooking time from coal.

Prepare the Site

Choose a source of fire of at least 8' from the bushes or any combustible materials. Make sure there are no hanging branches in the scene.

Use large stones or green stems to create a U-shaped circumference. If you use records, you need to check them from time to time. If the breeze blows, please face the wind behind the campfire.

A large stone is placed behind the stove as a chimney. "Chimney Rock" will help smoke and getaway.

Lay the Kindling

Fill the fire area with wrinkled paper or a fire.

Lay it down on the paper layer with the layer, each layer switching direction. Use chopped wood or small dry branches. Do not place the "conical tent pattern." The fire area must be completely covered with lighted chimneys.

Place a bucket of water near the fire zone. Turn the leaf to light a fire.

Build a Fire, Grade the Coals

When lit, add firewood. Wood should be as large as possible. Use solid or hard branches (if any). Distribute the wood evenly over the fire bed.

After the last flame has been extinguished, most of the remainder is white coal. Please use a stick to push the charcoal to the back end's top position and push the front end's bottom position to it. This will provide you with "Hi," "Med," and "Low" cooking settings. Or, iron the charcoal according to your preference.

For cooking, place the grill on the rocks or the damp green tree trunks. Place food directly on the grill or cooking utensils and prepare meals. If you cook directly on the grill, you can use a small spray bottle or spray gun to extinguish the rogue flame that usually occurs due to food distillation.

When the fire weakens, the coal is accumulated to get the most heat from it.

After cooking, add wood to the campfire at night. Before retiring, quench well and soak it in water. Place the stone on the fire bed. If necessary, it can be easily reassembled the next day.

What Wood to Use, Determine the Temperature of the Fire and Tricks

Cooking in a campfire requires clean, burning fire. This can only be done with dried and marinated wood. Trees that strip green woods in vain—fire can smoke, burn badly, and cause unnecessary pollution. If there is no dry wood, then it must be filled. Firewood is available in many public camps—please contact available firewood.

Ash

Fraxinus Mandshurica, or the most common ash, is the Yuleaceae family tree. There are about 50 different species, some are evergreen, and others are rough. Ash is considered one of the best firewood in the world. It burns easily, maintains very little moisture, and does not produce much smoke. These properties make them very suitable for use in campfires. Unlike other woods, white wax burns when it is green. If you find some ash around the camp, try burning it.

Cedar

If you want to build a burning fire to keep it warm, look for flammable cedarwood. The flame it produces is not as large as some other woods mentioned above, but it lacks the flame's size and is made of heat. Cedar produces excellent heat and is ideal for burning wood on cold nights. In addition, the cedar has a unique and pleasant aroma, which is not found anywhere else. Most people love this hidden and unique perfume. Of course, that's why some furniture polishes and other consumer products carry the scent of cedar.

The only drawback to beech is that it is heavy and takes some time to burn completely.

Black Cherry

Black cherry has low smoke and a unique aroma, which is easy to handle wood and is very suitable for different campsites. It provides moderate heat and cool sparks, so it is best to choose wood in summer or spring. You just need a gentle breeze to catch up with, and its lovely scent makes it perfect for you to smoke a piece of meat, fish or chicken in the camp kitchen.

Black cherry cannot provide the heat and light that other types of wood (such as beech) can provide, so it is not ideal for winter adventures.

Determine the Temperature of the Fire

Internal temperature: fire can reach an internal temperature of 1650 ° F (900 ° C) in a flame, which is called a continuous flame region.

Cooking temperature: above the flame where the flame is not visible (called the hot column region); the temperature can be expected to be around 600 ° F (320 ° C). This is where you cook. The further away from the flame, the lower the temperature.

Large campfires (such as campfires) may get hotter—more than 2,000 degrees Fahrenheit (1,100 ºC). Of course, you are not likely to cook over a full-size campfire.

A typical campfire will become hot enough to melt aluminum cans, but not a cast-iron frying pan.

You may have seen what happens when you put a soda can (aluminum alloy) in the fire—it will almost melt and disappear, except for the top and bottom parts of the soda can.

Variables Affecting the fire Temperature

Like all fires, the temperature varies with many factors.

Fuel type: wood type (softwood, hardwood and resin) and dry (sun-dried or green).

Fire size: the amount of fuel will affect the degree of fire.

Oxygen flow: the fire in a metal fire pit will not be at the same temperature as the fire with the continuous oxygen supply (a breeze or a blower pair).

A good fire contains three components: fuel, air, and heat. Long flammable fires are hotter to burn than well-prepared and stable fires, and this is what we do for cooking.

Ingredients to a Good Fire

You will need three things:

Tinder: small branches, dead leaves, etc., will quickly ignite and generate heat, and begin to burn more wood. Paper, cardboard, and flaming agents can also be used as a fire.

Kindle: a thicker wooden block that is easier to burn than the log block you placed on it. These branches can be larger, thicker, small branches or pieces of primary fuel, which peel off larger trunks. When it burns quickly, you will start to produce charcoal, which lays a good foundation for your fire.

Fuel: the larger and tougher wood that is placed on top usually requires more heat and flame to burn, but once it is burned, it will burn, which is an ideal fire for cooking.

For cooking, you need heat to cook steadily as it does at home. If you stack everything up and create a fiery hell at once, it might look impressive, but it's not perfect for cooking.

Heavy fire can reach 1650 °F (900 °C), and aluminum can melt—it will quickly chew wood supplies and burn food.

In order to cook, your fire must burn first and then create uniform coal.

Start with Tinder. The tin can heat up and ignite, and when it burns, it will generate enough heat for your bulk fuel.

When it burns, it resembles the top of the burner, forming an ideal uniform heat source, and you can change the temperature by adding more records.

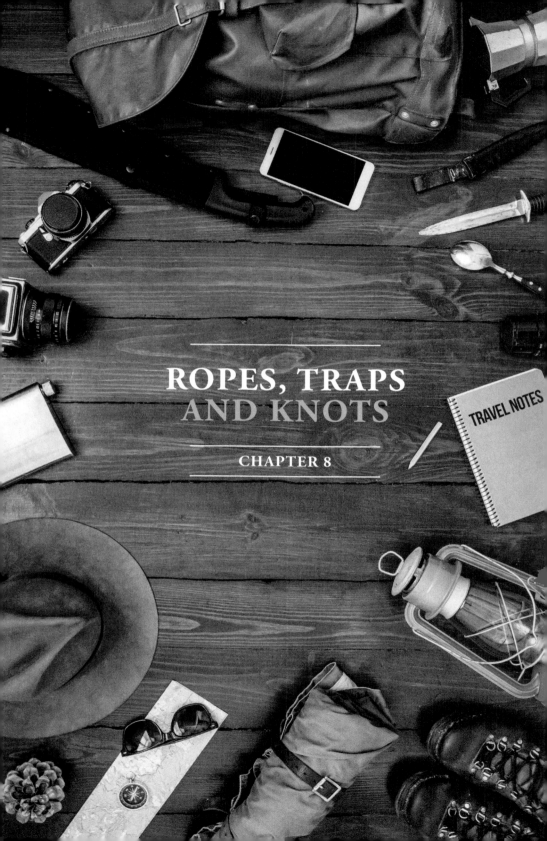

ROPES, TRAPS
AND KNOTS

CHAPTER 8

As part of any outdoor survival kit, you need to pack the necessary paraphernalia for making ropes, traps and knots.

If you find yourself in a survival situation, it is crucial that you be able to make ropes, traps and knots because they can mean the difference between life and death. When considering what items might be in your outdoo survival kit, it's just as important to add a few other things such as safety pins or needles that can help when working with plant fibers.

It's important that you know how to make ropes, traps and knots in the wilderness because they can help you with different tasks and at different times. For instance, if you need to construct a shelter or make a weapon, making these things with ropes can be vital.

Ropes are very useful items that you should have on hand in your survival kit at all times. Ropes come in handy for many things such as shelter building and securing items as well as building simple snares. In terms of building shelters, the rope allows you to build climbing ropes and other types of useful ladders when needed. The rope is also useful for making traps as well by using it to trap animals or small game.

Even if you don't plan on using ropes, it is still important to know how to make them because you never know when you might need some. It is vital that you know how to make a fishing line, which can be used for making traps or other useful purposes in the wilderness.

There are different types of rope that can be used depending on your needs and the situation at hand. Some ropes are made from fibers such as cotton, hemp and nylon while others are made from plant fibers such as green vines and bark.

If you are involved in a survival situation, being able to use the right kinds of ropes can also be important in various ways. The type of rope that you bring into the wilderness will depend on your needs.

In the woods we can find many different types of man-made traps. However, sometimes man-made traps are even more dangerous than natural ones such as live animals like snakes or large carnivores who have no fear of humans. While most of them perform the same function (such as a noose or a lasso) they are all used in different situations. When one is stuck in the woods and has to rely on medical, fire, or other man-made equipment it is very important that one knows how to tie these knots.

This knot makes anything done with any rope look very professional and also functions in rescue situations when one has to climb up slowly using their hands or other equipment. This knot is used in sport climbing. This will help you get down from a mountain safely if something happens to your climbing equipment.

This knot has many uses, but it is mainly used for rescue purposes and tools that require rope such as climbing equipment, pulleys, and lassos etc.. This knot has a wide variety of uses and is easy to tie and untie. It is made out of a loop in the rope or sometimes a metal snap link. This knot can be done in one hand but since it needs to be very tight and sometimes slides out, it is best done with both hands.

This knot works great for nets that one makes to capture animals or edible plants, but can also be used as a makeshift tent on trees/rocks, fishing net, or any other situation where one needs rope and in which they can't find proper materials. It is easy to learn to do this knot if you know how to do the square knot and will come in handy if you ever need it. It will save your life if you ever have to tie something with rope.

This knot can be used from a many different ropes. It is easy to learn and tie, but it is not used much due to its poor strength. However, it can be useful for some situations and it won't hurt if you don't have the proper materials anyway. This knot is suitable for most situations that you may encounter or need and other than that it isn't very useful, although there are times when it would come in handy for fishing or whatever other use you may need with this knot.

It is a temporary and very easy to tie knot which can be used in many situations. It can be used in many different things such as pouches, bags, or even large chairs or beds. It is easy to tie, but is slightly tuff to untie and it requires some patience.

What is Knot Tying

Knot tying is a fascinating practice. Tying knots is an essential skill required to take care of your equipment and clothing, and to repair them when they break down. It's also a lot of fun! Before you know it, you'll be tying new knots on the regular for no other reason than the satisfaction of having accomplished something that you couldn't before.

And no matter what your skill level, there's always a knot out there that you can discover. Don't be afraid to try new knots on your next trip out. When you do, watch the person tying them and see if they have any little tricks in mind that you can use.

When in an emergency situation, it is vital to know how to tie knots. Though these knots are often overlooked and underused, they can be a lifesaver when the need arises.

Knot tying is a skill of intricate design that has been used for centuries as one of the earliest forms of field communication.

A knot is a secure mechanical coupling made by interlocking two or more lengths of one or more types of flexible material to form an adjustable loop that is resistant to slipping, sliding, or other motions. It may also be tied with similar material in a series of loops or hitches around an anchor point. Knots are used primarily in three different ways: to attach ropes, lines, and cables; bind materials; and construct objects such as mats- a unique feature compared with other fastenings such as snaps and clasps.

In addition to practical uses on boats, in sailing, climbing, and hiking, knots also have symbolic uses in religion and literature. Knot reckoning is said to have been used by sailors as a means to determine their position at sea; a nautical mile was counted as one knot of speed through the water. Counting knots was an essential navigational skill needed in the days when there were no instruments such as magnetic compasses or sextants (devices used for taking angular measurements) that could be used from ships in order to find one's position at sea. This method of counting is still used today for measuring speed through water.

The origins of knot tying go back to ancient times. Over 5,000 years ago, humans fashioned the first knots for hunting, fishing, and clothing. Since then knots have been used to decorate objects and symbols.

Knot tying was very important in Asian martial arts in the past. The samurai wore their swords with two strings attached to a hilt as a symbolic reminder that they should always be prepared to face death—a reminder of their proper place as servants to the emperor.

How to make knots

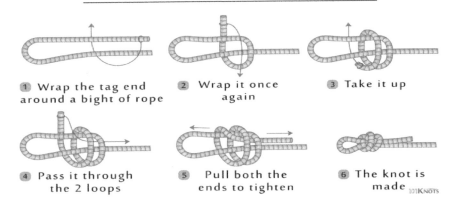

Poacher's Knot Instructions

① Wrap the tag end around a bight of rope

② Wrap it once again

③ Take it up

④ Pass it through the 2 loops

⑤ Pull both the ends to tighten

⑥ The knot is made 101KNOTS

Types of Knots

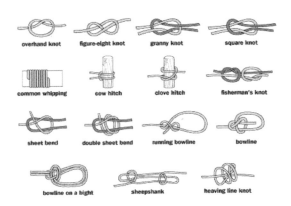

overhand knot   figure-eight knot   granny knot   square knot

common whipping   cow hitch   clove hitch   fisherman's knot

sheet bend   double sheet bend   running bowline   bowline

bowline on a bight   sheepshank   heaving line knot

113

Knot tying can be one of the most versatile and useful skills in a survival situation. If you have any aspirations of being an outdoorsman, even for weekend camping trips, knowing how to tie a knot could come in handy.

We'll take a look at what types of knots are available and how you can use them in different circumstances.

Many of these knots are simple to learn, and you'll be able to get the hang of them in no time. Let's dive right in!

Bends: These are the kinds of knots used for joining two ropes together. These might be the simplest knots to learn since they don't require any special techniques or maneuvers. Square Knot The square knot is a quick and easy way to join two ropes together. A square knot looks like an "x" on one end after it is tied. Double a Square Knot The same as the square knot above only it is often used when you need to tie two ropes together, but want to use less rope. This creates more space between the two pieces of rope. Hunter's Bend A hunter's bend, or fisherman's bend, is an easy way to join two pieces of rope. It can be used to shorten the length of one piece of rope without having to cut it. It has several other strengths and weaknesses that depend on how it is tied. Turk's Head This knot is used for decorative purposes and can also be used as a stopper knot that prevents ropes from passing through objects such as grommets or turnbuckles. The knot is also used to secure a boat's painter to a cleat.

Reef Knot: The Reef Knot also known as "figure 8 knot" because the knot looks like the number 8 may be the simplest possible way of tying two pieces of rope together. It also has many other uses that help prevent the knot from working loose during use. Double a "figure 8" Knot This knot is often used when joining two ropes together with no thought of anything else, but it can be tied into other things such as tent pegs or anything else you might want to tie onto a rope. "Albright Knot" its name is derived from Captain Herbert A. "Tim" Albright who popularized it in the Navy in 1942. It's a variation of the "clove hitch" (also known as the "Albright hitch") and is mainly used to attach a life jacket, net or lifeline to another object. But it's also useful when tying items such as tent pegs to a rope, but it's also very handy for holding a rope onto something or for joining two ropes together in other situations.

Bowline: This knot is best used when you want to tie something down and are worried about the item working loose. It can be used to tie things like tent pegs down or to secure an object such as a life ring onto an anchor point. It's also used to tie a rope around a cleat.

Palomar Knot: This is a knot that is often used by mountaineers. It's essentially used to wrap around the ridges of a mountain, or around other objects. It can also be used for tying life jackets onto people or for securing two ropes together, but it's mainly useful for creating a loop of rope or string that might be useful in other situations.

Slip Knot: Slip knots are widely used by anglers and hikers, but they can also be useful in another type of situation: tying down loose objects such as tent pegs or securing the end of a rope to something. They can also be used to make a loop on one end of a rope. The Slip Knot is widely known as the "Palomar knot" after the Mountain Rescue Service that popularized it in the 1950s. Palomar Knots are often used to tie down a tent peg, but they can also be used for joining two ropes together in an emergency situation where you don't want anything tied to a fixed point. The Palomar knot is tied by making two loops and then tying them together so they are either both standing up, or the left loop lies flat against the rope behind it. The double loop is then tied tightly to form the knot. Figure 8 Knot This knot is often used when tying a fishing net to a pole or when using a bowline in an emergency situation. It can also be used for joining two ropes together, but it's mainly useful for creating a loop of rope or string that might be useful in other situations.

Overhand Knot: The overhand knot is one of the most common knots tied by people. It's usually used for tying two ropes together and can be used as a stopper knot to prevent the rope from going through other objects such as turnbuckles or grommets. If you are tying a boat to a dock, it can also be used in this way. Overhand knots are also used to secure a life preserver onto a person and can be tied very easily, but they are often tied incorrectly if they are not tied in the right place. The overhand knot is often tied by using the thumb and forefinger of one hand and pulling the loop down over two fingers of the other hand.

Friction Hitch: The friction hitch is a simple bend which can be used as a stopper knot to prevent your rope from passing through objects like grommets or turnbuckles in a similar way to how an overhand knot works as a stopper, but it doesn't have any additional strength. The friction hitch stops your rope from passing through objects like turnbuckles by jamming it rather than holding it in place. This can lead to a situation where the friction hitch can become jammed inside the turnbuckle and get stuck, preventing you from undoing your knots. It's often used as a stopper knot for tying a rope down to an anchor point or something else.

Round Turn and Two Half Hitches: The round turn and two half hitches is similar to a friction hitch but is tied around an object rather than over the object. The half hitches can be used in different ways depending on what you are tying them around. For example, the ones above were tied around two pegs in a tent peg system so that when you pull on the rope, it would pull both pegs together. Round Turn Choker: The round turn choker is similar to a rounded turn but can be used in place of a friction hitch on a rope when you need to stop your rope from passing through objects like grommets or turning buckets and want a stronger hold than just jamming against them. It also produces a nice loop on the working end, which can be handy if you are using it to tie down a tent peg. Round turn and two half hitches are often used as a simple way to tie two things together in a situation when you don't have anything else to use.

Slipped Half Hitch: The Slipped Half Hitch is often used for tying rope or cable around an anchor point such as the eye of a winch. It can also be used in other situations where you need something tied tightly and are worried about it slipping off or coming undone. It is also often used in place of a friction hitch when you want a stronger hold. However, it can still be easily removed if necessary. The one above is tied so that the working end is first passed around the standing part of the standing half hitch, then pulled back through, and secured by passing it through the loop again to lock it in place. Stove Bend (or Bowline)

Stove Bend Knot: This knot is sometimes called a "Bowline" because of its shape. It's often used to tie things down but can also be used to join two ropes together in a similar way to how an overhand knot works, but it doesn't take any extra effort to tie. It's also sometimes used to tie two ropes together when you want something tied down but don't have anything else. Figure 9 Bowline Knot This can be tied in many ways, the one shown here being a popular way. The knot creates a loop of rope which can be used in many situations, and it's often tied incorrectly so that it won't tie properly. If you're using this kind of knot to join two ropes together then make sure that your knot is fully tightened up before tying it off. The rope is then pulled back through the loop to completely tighten the knot up, and then the end of the rope is secured by tying some webbing over it.

Tightening a Bowline Knot: Figure 10 Bowline Knot As the Bowline is tightened, and the working end of a rope runs in a figure 8 (or "buntline") around your body. If you are using this knot as part of an anchor system then make sure that you have a stronger body part to hold onto before tightening it down. If you buckle your knees together before tightening it down, for instance, then you can push with that knee until it gets tight enough to stop slipping out. Rigging System

Rope Ends: Rope ends are the ends of ropes where you can secure them with a knot. They are usually used for an anchor point such as the eye of a winch. They can be lashed onto the harness, or they can be lashed to other rope that is being used in an anchor system (for example, if you have a single line from a halyard that needs to attach to another rope or something else). Loops and Fittings

In this instance, you have a round turn followed by two half hitches which form an eye. The eye is then tied by passing the ends of both ropes through it, allowing enough play to fit over the other rope so that it can be tugged tight against itself. You then pass each end down through the eye and out again opposite sides of it to tighten up your knot. This can then be tied off on itself using the same two ropes. Make sure that your eye is large enough to fit over the other rope before you tighten it down. You can also have a square knot, which is considered to be more reliable than a round turn because it has less fiddliness, but is more time-consuming to tie. It also makes your rope ends thicker and bulkier if you use them to tie off other things in an anchor system. The square knot shown above could be used in the same way as a round turn followed by a half hitch, but the difference is that you would have one more visible part of your loop that people would see when travelling along it or inspecting it. Rope ends are the ends of ropes where you can secure them with a knot. They are usually used for an anchor point such as the eye of a winch. They can be lashed onto the harness, or they can be lashed to other rope that is being used in an anchor system (for example, if you have a single line from a halyard that needs to attach to another rope or something else).

Square Knot: The square knot is often referred to as "the king of knots" because it forms strong, secure knots and holds extremely well when tied properly. To tie the square knot you pass the working end around the standing part, then up and over the top to meet back down by your body. Then pass it through the loop on the other side of your body and out again on top. A line is then tied around it with a round turn knot, which forms an eye. Then a two half hitches knot is tied in the middle, and this forms the square knot. A second round turn is then tied around in the middle of the square knot and tightened up so that it can't easily be pulled out. This can then be attached to something else with some webbing or rope (if you want to make sure that it's secure, for example).

Double Half Hitch: This is usually used to tie two ropes together when you want something secured but don't have anything else available. It can also be used to tie something onto the end of a rope. Simply make sure that the two half hitches overlap each other slightly so that it doesn't come undone. It's also a good way to begin, or finish, many different knots because it gives you extra rope to play with and lets your knots be pulled in tighter because they are held in place by two parts of the hitch as opposed to one. The knot above is tied so that the working end passes around the standing part twice in a loop (or "round turn"), followed by passing it through the loop and then pulling back up through itself on top.

Figure 8 Loop: This is another way of joining ropes together when you don't have anything else available. It's made by passing the working end of one rope around its standing part, then up and over the top to meet back down by your body. Then pass it through the loop on the other side of your body and out again on top. This can then be tied off on itself using the same two ropes. Make sure that your loop is large enough to fit over the other rope before you tighten it down, or it will easily slip out during use.

Double Half Hitch: This knot is stronger than a "figure 8" loop but weaker than a strong overhand knot. It can be used when you don't have anything else available to tie the rope together, but you would choose an overhand knot if you wanted something that would hold very well.

Anchor Knot: The Anchor is a knot which is used to make sure that a rope end can't easily be pulled out of its place. It involves tying two parts of rope together with an overhand knot, so that it can't easily pull out of position or come undone in use. It also gives you more rope for additional attachments if it's tied properly. For example, if your anchor is tied too loosely then it will slip around in use, and if it's too tight then it won't work properly as an anchor. The knot used for this purpose should be a strong one, such as an overhand knot. This can also be used to tie two ropes together when you want something secured but don't have anything else available. It can also be used to tie something onto the end of a rope. Simply make sure that the two overhand knots overlap each other slightly so that it doesn't come undone. It's also a good way to begin, or finish, many different knots because it gives you extra rope to play with and lets your knots be pulled in tighter because they are held in place by two parts of the hitch as opposed to one.

Lark's Head: This is used to make a loop in the middle of a rope or to tie two ropes together. You can use it to attach the end of a rope to an anchor point, or you can use it in an anchor system where you want something (such as another rope) attached. It is usually made with softline or small diameter rope rather than large diameter ones because it will not hold well if the sheath of the line is too thick - such as when made with large diameter synthetic ropes. To tie a lark's head, pass the working end around your anchor point so that it comes up through its own hole from underneath. Then wrap it back around itself and pull tight. It's important to make sure that the rope overhand knot overlaps itself slightly to form the loop.

Hitch in a Slip Knot: This is similar to a square knot, although it's made with two half hitches tied in a row. It can be used to form multiple half hitches, or to form an anchor point. If you want some extra strength when tied you can also tie it so that it forms an "X" knot which will hold even more firmly than just two half hitches tied in opposite directions. Tie one end of your rope (in the loop) as for a square knot and pass that around the standing part of your rope twice (or three times). Then take it back through and around again so that it overlaps itself. Make sure that the rope overlaps onto itself, as this is a slip knot, otherwise it will not hold very well at all in use. Tighten up the knot and then tie a second half hitch by passing another length of rope through the loop on top of your first loop. This again should overlap onto itself. Tighten up the knot and then tighten up the first half hitch knot to make sure that the two halves overlap properly. You could also add a second half hitch if you wanted to.

Two Half Hitches: One end of your rope is tied as for a square knot and passed over your standing part twice (or three times). Then take it back through and around again so that it overlaps itself. Make sure that the rope overlaps onto itself, as this is a slip knot, otherwise it will not hold very well at all in use. Tighten up the knot and then tie a second half hitch by passing another length of rope through the loop on top of your first loop. This again should overlap onto itself. Tighten the knot and then tighten up the first half hitch knot to make sure that the two halves overlap properly. You could also add a second half hitch if you wanted to.

COPING WITH
BAD WEATHER

CHAPTER 9

It has been stated that unless you have survived the elements of nature, you are not really equipped to withstand any tragedy. When exposed to certain extremes, the human body is fragile and will only be able to resist them for a short period of time before breaking down. In this chapter, you will learn how to defend yourself from some of the factors discussed in the previous chapter. It is vital to remember that some of these survival strategies are not intended to be used for lengthy periods of time in high temperatures. Furthermore, if you find yourself trapped without the necessary tools or supplies, there isn't much you can do to remedy the situation. As a result, it is critical to seek refuge in a secure location and remain there until relief arrives.

Surviving in Extremely Cold Conditions

The coldest temperatures are the greatest cause of mortality in the majority of natural catastrophes. It is only within a very narrow range of temperatures that the human body is capable of functioning effectively before it starts to shut down. It is vital to note that hypothermia may occur much before the actual freezing point is reached. Hypothermia happens when your body begins to lose heat at a quicker rate than it is able to generate. This leads to a hazardous decrease in your core temperature, which may lead to death if not treated immediately. There are several ways in which freezing may result in death. First and foremost, the body's core temperature drops below normal levels, causing blood vessels to constrict. It becomes more difficult for your heart to pump blood throughout your body as a result of this. Shivering and exhaustion are possible side effects of this process.

Shivering is a natural mechanism for your body to generate heat by contracting and relaxing its muscles. As the temperature drops, you'll notice that you're shivering more and more violently. Over time, your muscles grow weary and finally quit functioning entirely.

When your muscles stop functioning, your body's capacity to generate heat diminishes as well. The following survival advice should be kept in mind if you find yourself stuck without enough clothes or shelter.

The human body can create enough heat to keep itself comfortable when at rest, provided it is properly covered and not exposed to the elements such as the wind. Due to the fact that the earth will take your body heat, it is critical to insulate yourself from the ground. This may be accomplished by sleeping on a cot or sleeping pad and enveloping oneself in a thermal reflective blanket, to name a few options. Water makes up between 50-75 percent of your body's composition, and even the act of drinking may cause your core temperature to rise. It is critical to locate fresh, flowing water if at all feasible since this will aid in the maintenance of your body's temperature. If you are attempting to elevate your core temperature, it is recommended not to consume alcoholic beverages or eat snow since both will pull heat away from your body.

During the winter, the easiest approach to locate water in a cold area is to seek it in the vicinity of green foliage. In addition, since frozen rivers and streams are regularly nourished by melting snow and ice, you may dig into the banks of frozen rivers and streams by digging into a low location in the river bank. This low point, as well as the middle of frozen lakes and ponds, are excellent places to look for water. It is important to remember that your core temperature must be increased to a safe level before hypothermia may take your life. If you find yourself trapped without shelter, it is critical that you remove yourself from the wind and out of any wet clothing as soon as possible, cover yourself in a thermal reflective blanket, and seek shelter from the weather. If you are in the company of someone who is suffering from hypothermia, you must keep them warm until assistance comes.

Surviving in Extremely Hot Conditions

As you may be aware, heat may kill more rapidly than cold in certain situations. It is the fact that your body is engineered to expel heat via the surface of your skin that makes overheating the most hazardous situation. Increased blood flow to the skin when you grow warm, clinging to the surface in an effort to cool you down. You will begin to perspire abundantly as soon as this occurs. We are experiencing a natural response meant to keep us alive during moments of extreme temperature. Unfortunately, while you are alone in the outdoors, your perspiration can attract insects, which may create serious difficulties if you are not careful. Here are some ideas for surviving the elements in hot areas that will enable you to be safe and healthy. Keeping your body temperature under control before it becomes dangerously high is the most effective strategy to fight to overheat. Finding shade or protection from the sun is an excellent approach to do this.

Whether you're climbing a mountain or just strolling through flat country, it's crucial to dress in light clothes that will allow your body to cool down as you exert yourself. Keeping the light out of your eyes is another benefit of wearing sunglasses, which allows you to better control your body temperature. If you are unable to go into the shade for whatever reason, you must wear light-colored clothing to ensure that some of the sun's rays are reflected back to you. Taking a refreshing plunge in a natural body of water that includes fish or other animals is one of the most effective methods to cool yourself. Riverbeds and streams should be avoided since they may be home to snakes, scorpions, and other critters that you do not want to come face to face with.

In order for your body to operate effectively, it needs a steady supply of fresh, clean drinking water. It's crucial to note that heated conditions rapidly dehydrate your skin, increasing the pace at which you lose water via your pores.

Keep in mind that the color of your urine may change depending on how hydrated you are at any one time. If it is light in color, there is a significant probability that you are not getting enough water into your system. If the color of your urine is black, it indicates that you have been dehydrating for an extended period of time, which may place additional pressure on your body during the hot summer months. If you find yourself in a hot area where it is difficult to acquire freshwater, you may manufacture your own by collecting water from the trees in your immediate vicinity. Cut the bark off any tree to get access to the moisture contained therein, which may be sucked straight into your mouth or utilized for other reasons in a survival scenario if it is available. A canteen or bottle of water is a smart idea to have on hand if you are traveling to a region that is renowned for its high temperatures and dry climate. Perspiration causes your body to lose a significant quantity of water, so knowing how your body responds in hotter conditions can help you decide how much water you need.

When your body starts to overheat, you must take urgent action to prevent more damage. If you are lost or stranded in a hot environment with no access to shade or water, it is vital that you locate both as soon as possible. Following your successful search for shelter and potable water, the next stage is to learn how to control your breathing so that you do not get overheated. Take a few calms, deep breaths, and try to relax as much as you possibly can. If you are working hard to construct a shelter or start a fire, take frequent pauses to allow your muscles to rest and cool down. Once the worst of the heat has gone, you should be able to return to your previous activities without experiencing too much damage.

A Few Pointers and Tricks

While camping, it is important to take excellent care of your body, especially your skin. This includes the removal of any unneeded piercings and other metal devices that may rip the skin and cause damage if anything goes wrong with the procedure. It also entails washing your clothing on a regular basis and bathing yourself on a sponge to keep yourself clean. You should try to dry yourself as much as possible before going to bed if you become wet. If you do this, you will limit the amount of moisture in your sleeping bag, which will lessen the likelihood of mildew or mold developing. When camping, you should never consume untreated water, regardless of whether it comes from a natural source or a man-made one. GIARDIA lamblia and other dangerous microbes may cause severe disease or even death if they are not treated promptly. While camping, there are a variety of options for treating the water you use. Among the most frequent methods, boiling is the most effective since it kills practically every sort of noncore-forming germ known to man. Iodine is also efficient against a wide range of bacteria, viruses, and cysts, all of which may create difficulties in the digestive system when consumed in sufficient quantities. Despite the fact that the vast majority of insects are harmless or even useful to you, it is always a good idea to protect yourself against bug bites. Insects may carry diseases that can make you extremely ill if they bite you, while others just possess an unpleasant venom that can be irritating to the skin. If you're camping in the woods, wear long trousers and tuck them into your socks at night, especially if there's a good chance that insects will be around. If you're camping in the open air, make use of bug repellent and keep your tent as tightly closed as possible to avoid being bitten by mosquitoes. There are various things that you can do to ensure that your shelter is secure and pleasant throughout the year. These include: When it's chilly outside, you may use straw or leaves to help keep drafts at bay by insulating the floor.

Maintain a roaring fire outdoors to lessen the likelihood of bringing hazardous species inside your shelter from the outside. Cover the tarp with leaves, dirt, or other natural materials to block rainfall and melting snow from getting inside the shelter. Fill up any cracks or openings in your shelter with leaves, straw, and other material to keep the elements out. Several measures may be taken to avoid hypothermia if the temperature lowers and you find yourself chilly and wet: Locate or construct a fire so that you may warm yourself and dry off after your swim. Get inside your shelter and pile on numerous layers of blankets, fabric, bark, or anything else that will provide insulation to keep the cold out. Wet garments should be wrung out and put back on as soon as possible if you do not have any warm clothes to wear. It is preferable to be cold than to become a victim of hypothermia. Going on a camping vacation should never be done without carrying along with equipment that will assist you in surviving in the worst-case situation.

You should always be prepared, even if you feel there is no danger to you. It is better to be safe than to risk damage or death just because you did not carry the necessary equipment with you. Keep an extra lighter and waterproof match in a sealed container on hand just in case your first one fails. Ensure you have a fire starter and enough fuel to kindle a fire regardless of the weather conditions. Having the skill to build a fire can assist you in many ways, including staying warm, cooking food, purifying water, keeping insects away, keeping wild creatures at bay, signaling for aid, and many other things. Ensure you have tools such as bait rods, fishing line, hooks, snares, traps, pots and pans, knives of various sizes, and lamps or lanterns with additional batteries with you when you go fishing.

If you sprain or break a bone, you'll also need mirrors for signaling and first aid kits with pain relievers like ibuprofen or aspirin, which might be the difference between life and death if you're in serious agony.

Even if you are camping in the country, near to your house, there is still the possibility of injury or death due to the fact that you are exposed to the elements for the whole night. Always be on the lookout for possible hazards, no matter how implausible they may seem to be at the moment. It is not recommended to fall asleep over a campfire. Keep it under control at all times, and make certain that no combustible materials are in the area. Please only use it for heat when you are awake; this includes preparing meals, cooking, and boiling water. During the day, keep your distance from potentially deadly creatures such as snakes or bears if you are in their region. Keep a light on at all times throughout the night so that they are aware of your presence and do not approach your shelter. In the event that someone approaches your camp in search of food or water, you should not allow them in unless you know them personally or have been informed that visitors are permitted to stop by. Stranger danger is just as present in a survival crisis as it is when you are merely walking around your neighborhood at night.

Camping is enjoyable and may help you appreciate the beauty of nature, but it is critical that you learn how to live in the wilderness before venturing out into the wilderness on your own. Keep in mind what to do if someone becomes lost or injured, as well as what risks to be on the lookout for at all times. Keep in mind what goods are essential for your safety and how to build your shelter in order to better protect yourself from the weather. Spending time now mastering these abilities might be the difference between returning home alive and becoming another tale in the newspaper later on down the road.

FIRST AID
OUTDOOR FIRST AID KIT

CHAPTER 10

We all know what to do when we get hurt: call an ambulance, go to the emergency room, and wait patiently for medical care. However, what if you were stranded in a remote area and couldn't get help? What about minor injuries like twisted ankles or cuts that need a few stitches? In the event that one of your adventures goes awry or you're feeling underprepared for summer camping trips, check out this list of first-aid supplies every outdoor enthusiast should have.

1. First Aid Kit

These kits vary considerably in size and contents, but they all contain an assortment of supplies like gauze dressings, Band-Aids, antibiotic ointment, tweezers for removing splinters (or other objects), medical tape (for tying off wounds) and other first-aid supplies. Most kits will also contain items that are more for comfort, like pain relievers, cough drops, anti-diarrhea medication, hand sanitizer and more.

2. Emergency Blanket

While many of us may not think of ourselves as being cold-blooded animals, most people would die without access to a blanket to keep warm. These blankets tend to be lightweight and extremely durable and can be used for warmth or shelter.

3. Hydration Bladder

A hydration bladder is a large container filled with water that you can strap to a pack or use in a survival situation to keep yourself hydrated for up to 24 hours. They're particularly useful when backpacking or camping in areas where there's no reliable access to drinking water, and they're also great for things like boating, hiking and running. They come in a variety of sizes, from 7-11 ounce bladders that weigh less than half an ounce, which are the most common size, down to 50-liter bladders that can hold close to 20 gallons of liquid. Some of these bladders are collapsible, some are not. Some are available with attached drinking tubes and some are not.

4. Trauma Shears

Not all doctors carry these, but they're an invaluable tool when you're the one doing the cutting. Trauma shears are useful for cutting bandages, splints, webbing and any other type of material that you'd need to cut in emergency situations. They're particularly useful if you have a wound on your arm or leg as they make it easier to expose the flesh beneath the damaged skin as opposed to cutting around a bandage or dressing.

5. Eyepatch

Aside from their obvious use as a way to protect your eye from dirt and debris, eyepatches serve a second purpose – they make you look tough. They're especially handy to have when you're going hiking or skiing if you want to protect the skin around your eyes from rubbing against the material of your helmet. While they can be costly, $10 for an eye patch is nothing compared to the expense of getting out of work or school with an injury because of something stupid like losing an eyeglass.

6. Paracord

Paracord is an incredibly versatile material that's available in many different colors, strengths and sizes. It can be used to attach things like carabiners, fishing line or even survival bracelets to your pack. It can also be used as a bandage for small cuts and scrapes, wrapped around objects like tent pegs to hold them in place or threaded through clothing for extra warmth or to make adjustments. There are over 20 different uses for this handy little piece of kit!

7. Duckbill Mouthpiece

This handy accessory is perfect for water purification systems like the Sawyer Mini which makes it easier to drink without tossing out contaminated water. It provides an airtight seal to the drinking tube, so you'll be able to drink with less water entering your mouth. This can also be used as a barrier between high pressure water sources and your face, like when jumping into a river or lake.

8. BackBrace

This is another accessory that you wouldn't think of but would benefit from having in this situation. A backbrace will keep the damaged area of your back stabilized while you're waiting for help, easing pressure on the muscles and ligaments that may be stretched out by simply sitting or laying down. It allows you to rest with full use of your arms and legs without putting too much weight on the affected area.

9. Chlorine Dioxide Tabs

These tabs are great for emergency disinfecting of water sources like lakes, streams and ponds. They'll eliminate 99.9% of viruses and bacteria in contaminated water within a few minutes, so you can have safe drinking water without having to boil it in a pot. They're perfect for situations where you don't have a stove handy or you don't have access to camp fuel in order to boil the water. They're also great when you're camping near a pond that's been contaminated by heavy rains or other factors that could introduce animal or human feces into the water which isn't good for swimming in but is fine to drink if filtered properly.

10. Survival Doolie

It doesn't matter if you're right and no one else sees the error of their ways. If your campfire has the chance to ignite dry brush or overhanging trees, all you need to do is pull out your survival blanket and do what you can to contain the fire. Having a lightweight waterproof bag like this one will help stop fire from spreading and not allow it to reach dry brush or other flammable materials that could reignite when wet.

11. Handheld GPS

A handheld GPS is incredibly useful for outdoor adventures, whether you're driving through the mountains, hiking through the forest or enjoying a picnic in the park. With enough satellites overhead, most handheld GPS units will be able to plot your location on a map with great precision so you can see exactly where you are in relation to nearby landmarks. This is important when things go wrong and you need help getting out of the wilderness so rescuers can find you easily.

12. Survival Whistle

A standard survival whistle measures about 3 inches in length and has a lot of power behind it. Most survival whistles are made from aluminum or plastic and they can be heard from long distances which allows you to signal for help even if you're out of sight. The blast from a whistle can travel much farther than a human voice, especially through a forest or across open fields. They're also very useful for signaling for help while you're trapped in your car or cabin.

13. Waterproof Shelf Ties

These ties, which come in a variety of colors and styles, can be used to hold signs and small items like maps and compasses on your outdoor adventure. They're also great when you need to dry something quickly from an overflowing water source because they'll easily absorb the water from whatever they're tied around without affecting the materials underneath it. They can be used to keep loose items from floating away in the water or always keep your team members together during a hike.

14. Micro-Light

This little light packs a punch in terms of brightness, running on just two AA batteries. It has three settings, bright, brighter and brightest so you can select which one works best for your needs. When buying a Micro-Light, make sure you get the style that has the button on top because it makes switching between the different settings much easier. Make sure it has a lanyard attached to it so you can hook it onto your keychain or clothing. A Micro-Light is useful for signaling to rescuers when you're stuck or lost or if your campsite is too dark to read by at night.

BASE CAMP FIRST-AID KIT

This kit design is for the needs of multiple people within the same group. Trained responders may wish to substitute elements to better suit their needs according to their level of training.

Protect any sterile dressings within your kit from moisture by sealing them in 1-gallon freezer bags in groups of four.

Your kit should always be easily accessible and its location known by everyone in your group.

A designated person, typically the one with the most training, should be appointed medical person in charge.

Label all containers clearly and include instructions in case the medical person in charge is the one who becomes injured.

Splints can be improvised in the field from natural material or foam sleeping pads. So only include SAM splints if you have space or the desire to carry them.

BANDAGES AND DRESSINGS

4" × 4" gauze pads

2" × 2" gauze pads

3" gauze roller bandage

Paper tape

Elastic roller bandage

Self-adhering bandage

Cravat

Adhesive bandages (various sizes)

Steri-Strips or butterfly bandages

Wound irrigation syringe

11/2" athletic tape

2nd Skin

Moleskin

OINTMENTS AND MEDICATIONS

Povidone iodine

Triple antibiotic cream

Cortizone cream

Aspirin

Ibuprofen

Acetaminophen

Diphenhydramine (antihistamine)

Hydration salts/Jell-O

TOOLS

Bandage scissors/EMT shears

Thermometer with hard case

Tweezers

Nitrile gloves

Sawyer Extractor

Notepad and pencil

Small multitool or Swiss Army knife

Emergency space blanket

Safety glasses and face shield

AIRWAY DEVICES

CPR mask

Nasopharyngeal airway

SIGNAL DEVICES

Signal mirror

Road flare

Headlamp and batteries

Learning CPR

People die every day and it is your responsibility to help save someone's life. It's not always easy and the first time you might not know what to do, but CPR will help you figure out what each step of the process entails. This chapter gives some tips on how to learn CPR so you can save a life if an emergency happens.

Learn CPR: How to Learn the Skill

Learning anything new is difficult, even with regular instruction, but learning a skill like CPR takes more than just knowledge of that skill — it also takes practice and patience. You need to find ways of studying and practicing without worrying about running into classmates or getting caught up in distractions like TV or music.

Here are some ways you can learn CPR on your own:

Practice on a doll or plush animal. You can't do this in class so you'll have to learn the skill at home. Learn how to open the animal's mouth and seal your lips around it so you can pretend to give compressions. Make sure the toy has a hole for breathing so you don't suffocate it before completing all 30 compressions.

You can't do this in class so you'll have to learn the skill at home. Learn how to open the animal's mouth and seal your lips around it so you can pretend to give compressions. Make sure the toy has a hole for breathing so you don't suffocate it before completing all 30 compressions. Practice on a stuffed animal toy. This gives an easier way to practice CPR without worrying about hurting a living being.

This gives an easier way to practice CPR without worrying about hurting a living being. Go to a quiet, empty space and practice on a doll or stuffed animal without first opening its mouth to release air from the lungs. Do not push down past her chest as this can cause cardiac arrest and death quickly, so instead use your hands to press firmly on her heartbeat as you perform the other steps of CPR.

Do not push down past her chest as this can cause cardiac arrest and death quickly, so instead use your hands to press firmly on her heartbeat as you perform the other steps of CPR. Practice on a doll or stuffed animal by first opening its mouth and then tying a piece of cloth around its face.

Wilderness First Aid Tips and Tricks

Most people probably don't know it, but there are lots of practical wilderness first aid tips and tricks. Many of these are highly-effective ways to handle emergencies when you're out in the woods or mountains. These tactics will help save lives if they're followed correctly:

-Know what to do and how to do it: know the ABCs and use a pocket guide.

-Map your route: it's easy for an injured hiker to get lost on unfamiliar terrain.

-Leave a travel route behind you so rescuers don't have to guess where you were headed before things went wrong.

-Communicate with your search party: let them know exactly where you are, and how long ago you were there.

-Always carry a first-aid kit: it could save your life if you get hurt out in the woods, or if someone else hurts themselves while they're helping someone else.

-Carry a small flashlight, whistle, and map to orient yourself at night.

-Carry extra water for yourself and the injured person if you're hiking through rough country.

-Don't use smoke signals or flares to call for help; anyone trying to find you might mistake smoke signals for forest fires. (Instead, make noise with rocks like clapping hands. Throwing stones onto a tree trunk is also effective, but remember that it might attract predators.) Easier still, yell to draw attention to yourself.

-Don't move the injured person unless you have to.

-Keep the injured person calm and conscious if they're unconscious: get out your lights and call out where you are. (This tip alone will probably save more lives than any of the others mentioned here. It's amazing how often people don't stop and do this.) Never move a patient without first checking for and treating high-risk injuries like long bone breaks and head trauma.

-Stay calm: if an injured person panics, they're more likely to injure themselves further. Often, people who get into trouble in the backcountry end up injuring themselves because they say or do the wrong thing (or don't say anything at all).

-If you need to carry an injured person, put weight on their legs, not their back. You can lift someone onto a litter or stretcher without hurting them as much as if you lift them onto their back.

-If you're going to give fluids by mouth, do it from a bottle. Never feed from a bottle with a straw because a panicked person might suck the fluid back into your mouth and choke you.

-If you need to move an injured person, keep their head and neck stabilized. (This tip doesn't count if they've been knocked unconscious.)

-Store any medications in waterproof bags. Water can destroy medicine that isn't stored properly.

-Be careful! Avoid trips and slips that could injure you or the people around you at home or in the field.

-Stay out of trouble.

I hope that this list helps you when you're in the wild. If you can, always use a map and compass to find your way back to safety. Always carry a first-aid kit with bandages, tape, a thermometer, sterile water, and extra tubing and gauze in case of emergencies. People have been saved from heart attacks by taking an aspirin every 15 minutes when they're hiking late at night .

If you're a kid, don't forget to keep a whistle with you. You can often get someone's attention by blowing on it like you're calling for help (and if they're close, they'll hear it).

Also, remember that you can always try making noises on purpose; there are lots of places that will echo the sounds of voices or rocks hitting trees. Think about where those places are and plan your route accordingly. Be prepared for the worst, but also stay positive. No one can know what will happen next, but if you follow these tips, you'll be ready to act quickly if something does go wrong.

Find Useful Object in Nature

There is no denying that outdoor survival skills are a must-have, especially if you live in either the wilderness or in a less than desirable urban location. These days we have more access to survival skills than ever before, thanks to the internet and technology. However, they can be hard to find sometimes when you need them most! For example, how can you prepare for an emergency - or even practice your backcountry skills - without access to land?

Fortunately there are ways around this issue by utilizing items found throughout nature. These items, more often than not, are found everywhere depending on where you look. There are many items that can be used to perform simple tasks or provide a measure of comfort in adverse circumstances (like improvised tents). Some of these items may be able to solve a multitude of problems ranging from creating a makeshift shelter from sticks and leaves to providing warmth during the colder months.

This list is by no means comprehensive, however there are certain tools and techniques that are easier to find than others when it comes to survival in the wilderness. In fact, learning how to utilize these items might give you an advantage over other survivors who haven't learned this vital skill set.

Pine Needles

Pine needles can be used to make a bed in the mud or snow. They also make an excellent emergency fire starter, even when wet. There are a number of ways that they can also be utilized in other emergency situations as well. Check out these awesome

Pine Needle Survival Tips right here on Survivalist Prepper!

Cotton Balls/Bee Stings

Cotton balls and bee stings have a multitude of uses and their uses are only limited by your imagination. They can be used to start a fire, treat wounds and even break up kidney stones. Keep in mind that cotton balls do not burn very well and are a bit more difficult to start a fire. However, these can be used as 'filler' in an improvised tinder bundle.

Bark

If you are looking to start a fire, don't waste your time with flint and steel. Look around and locate some bark that has shaded its side. Shaping the bark into a rough point is all that is needed to create sparks that can start a fire. If a fire is not needed, the bark can also be used to protect wounds from further infection by helping to stop bleeding and keeping out germs.

Pinecones

Pinecones make excellent water filters as they are porous and allow water to flow through them easily. Be sure to crush up some of the smaller pieces in order for it to filter as effectively as possible.

Tobacco/Tobacco Pouches/Packaging

If you are going to use tobacco, it makes sense to try and re-use the packaging for other things. These types of products can be used as a way to start a fire, store food or even help stop bleeding if needed.

Dried Leaves

Dried leaves are an excellent source of food and can be eaten raw, boiled or even roasted. It should be noted that leaves will have to be thoroughly dried in order for them to be edible after exposure to moisture. Dried leaves can also make for a great form of shelter if you're seeking protection from the elements like rain and snow.

Leaves

Leaves are a natural form of insulating material that could act as a temporary sleeping bag or tarp when needed. They are fairly thick and compact, making them able to be used as a sort of 'home away from home'.

Fork/Knife

The fork is an obvious choice but it's still useful to know how to use one if needed. You don't want to use the tines as a place for food, however they are great for digging or clearing out debris. The point of the fork can also be used to start a fire if you're starving and desperate.

Hobo Stove

The hobo stove is an excellent way to cook food over an open flame. It's compact, easy to make and very durable too. You can gather up materials in almost any location where trees grow and use them to create a safe cooking environment for yourself with little effort.

Snail Shells

Snail shells can be used to hold water or small amounts of food if needed. They can also be used as vessels for boiling water that are virtually indestructible in most situations. They can also be placed on top of a reed stalk and used as a way to direct the smoke from a fire upwards if you're trying to make it visible to searchers. If you are lost and unable to reach the surface, this technique will help searchers locate your position not only with air but with sound too!

Bamboo Stalks

Bamboo is one of the most versatile plants in nature and shouldn't be overlooked. It can be used in the construction of shelters, fishing poles and if you're lucky enough to come across a hollow stalk it could even be used for storing items or as a flute.

Cactus Spines

Cactus spines can be used when nothing else is available to spear food or even as part of an emergency fishing kit. Be sure to remove the needles first!

Thorns

In certain cases where food is needed, thorns make an excellent hunting tool. They can also be utilized when creating an improvised shelter by hammering them into the ground and covering them with whatever leaves are on hand.

Reed Protrusions

Reed protrusion can be used to trap small animals such as mice and even acts as effective tinder for catching a fire when needed. It can also be used as bushcraft decorations but it should be noted that if you're using them for shelter, they will give you little but insulation. In many cases, the only benefit is that they are easy to hide in and make for excellent camouflage.

Bamboo Reeds

Bamboo reeds have a number of uses that should not be overlooked by any means. They make excellent fishing poles, canoes and even serve as emergency shelters in certain situations if nothing else is available. The best use of them, however, is as part of a fire kit. You can cut them up into sections and then insert a piece of your tinder in the center to create a small fire that will help you to boil water on the spot.

Rocks/Pebbles

Rocks or Pebbles are useful when it comes to starting fires. However, they are not very hot explosives so they should not be overlooked in any situation that needs more than just smoke blowing around. It would be best to use them in conjunction with another type of explosive however, as they release a decent amount of heat when struck together.

Sticks/Branches

Sticks and branches can be used to help construct small shelters or even used as walking sticks. They can also be fashioned into makeshift shovels if you are in the middle of a blizzard with no other form of excavation tool available.

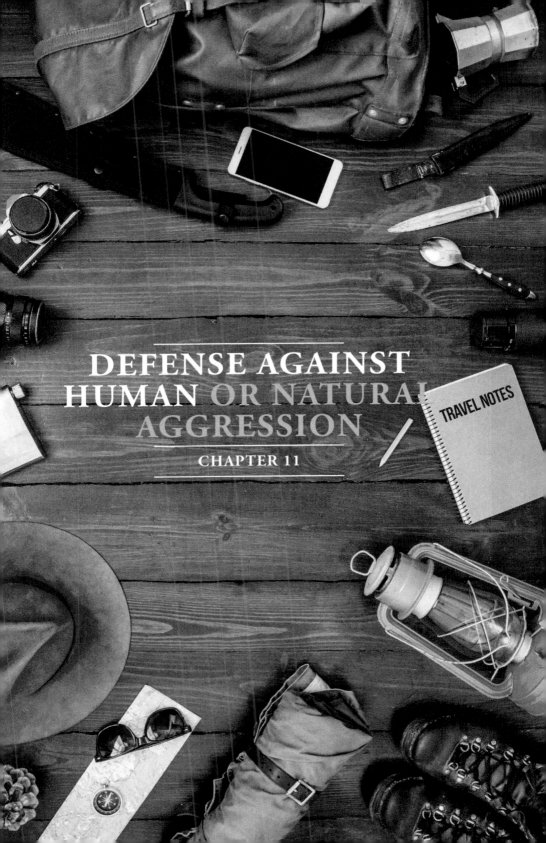

DEFENSE AGAINST HUMAN OR NATURAL AGGRESSION

CHAPTER 11

Whether you're an urbanite or a wilderness expert, the tips will help you cope with any situation that comes your way. Learn how to build an emergency kit, survive outdoors without food or water, escape from any vehicle after an accident on icy roads.... the list goes on and on! Memorize these instructions and keep them in mind for when they might come in handy.

1. Always have a fire extinguisher close at hand in case of an emergency.

2. Locate an escape route from your home or office building if fire blocks access to the door or window.

3. Having enough food, water, and necessary supplies for a week's worth of meals is a must for each person in your household.

4. Keep a list of all the information you might need to make calls in an emergency and keep it tucked away somewhere safe and easy to access.

5. Practice how you'll pick up your children from school in a large-scale emergency.

6. Test all smoke detectors in your home with a new battery to ensure they're still functional.

7. Be sure that you know where the nearest fire escape is located.

8. Always keep some kind of survival tool on hand to protect yourself if you feel threatened as you leave the house every day.

9. Keep a sharp knife in your car and always have a pair of pliers within reach if you need to make repairs or escape from your vehicle.

10. Keep at least one handgun on hand at all times for personal protection.

11. Create and practice a plan of action for an evacuation.

12. Measure each member of the family and record their height and weight on multiple occasions throughout the year to create an accurate survival kit for each individual based on their specific needs.

13. Try to create or join an emergency preparation community.

14. Be sure to record all family members' fingerprints on a CD or some other small and easy-to-carry device if you have to evacuate quickly and cannot locate your children.

15. Always carry a small piece of paper with all the essential numbers for your family.

16. Know how to make a splint and how to help someone who's been injured in an accident.

17. Write down the name and numbers of your neighbors so that you can quickly contact them in case of an emergency.

18. Prepare a bear-proof garbage container.

19. Make sure your smoke detector is stored at least six inches above the floor for it to work correctly.

20. Always keep a can of bear spray or pepper spray in your vehicle.

21. Know how to prepare and handle wild games.

22. Know how to make an emergency shelter.

23. Make sure you know how to prepare a fire using multiple methods and different starting materials.

24. Time yourself while taking an emergency preparedness course.

25. Ensure you have the proper tools to survive in the wilderness.

26. Practice how you'll get out of a car if it's caught on fire (i.e., unbuckling your seatbelt if it's buckled incorrectly, unbuckling your child's seatbelt, or removing their car seat if needed).

27. Keep a working fire extinguisher in your kitchen.

28. Learn how to use a fire blanket to control small fires.

29. Know how to use your car's emergency brake and a hand brake for manual vehicles.

30. Keep a knife or razor blade in your first aid kit for cutting bandages if you don't have scissors handy.

31. Keep an empty cardboard box with all of the supplies needed for the baby's first aid kit in case there's an emergency, and you need to be able to rush the baby off to the hospital immediately

32. Learn how to check the fluid levels in your car's radiator and turn off your vehicle if you notice the liquid level is too high.

33. Ensure you know how to spot warning signs for a possible gas leak.

34. Keep potassium iodide tablets in your house for protection against nuclear radiation or nuclear war.

35. Ensure you know how to turn a car's engine off in case of an accident.

36. Know how to remove the tire from your car if the rim breaks and you need to change your tire.

37. Learn how to remove and dispose of handcuffs.

38. Know how to use a fire extinguisher if it's provided on your residence or business.

39. Ensure you've checked your car for any possible hazards that could blow up.

40. Make sure you have flashlights and extra batteries around your house.

41. Have a working smoke alarm in your home.

42. Learn how to use a universal blood type card if you or one of your children are lost and needs to be identified.

43. Learn how to clean up a bloody wound in the event of an accident.

44. Know what to do if you're lost.

45. Understand how to escape out of a store or building that catches on fire.

46. Learn how to treat a heart attack (Call 911, have the person lie down, and raise feet 8 inches off the ground or lower back if possible).

47. Know what to do after performing CPR.

48. Learn how to perform first aid on bleeding wounds.

49. Know what to do if someone falls on a snowy road.

50. Understand the difference between burning and freezing water.

Tips on How to Escape From the Wilderness

Maintaining a sense of safety while traversing the Great Outdoors is essential for any adventurer. There are many situations that the nature lover may encounter where they find themselves lost, stranded, or worse.

Before we go too far, let us state the obvious. The techniques outlined are not foolproof. They all have their risks and should be used only by those truly confident that they can avoid danger. If you're not one of those people, take note: stay at home. This could be your last chance to determine if you're an outdoorsman or a dinosaur.

1) Make a fire. A fire can keep predators at bay as well as provide warmth. Search for dry wood and collect dead grasses and leaves to get a good blaze going quickly.

2) Keep warm. Keeping warm is the most important thing you can do. While a fire is going, make sure to build up the fire as much as possible and sit near it with your back to the heat.

3) Eat only what you can carry.

4) Lock your car. This is the best idea since eating a box of raisins if you're not familiar with automotive locks.

5) Get creative. This is where things get serious. You never know what you'll find along the way for survival needs. The more creative your ideas, the better off you'll be, and the less chance that someone else will beat you to it.

6) Make a make-shift knife.

7) Find shelter. Finding shelter will help keep you warm and dry. Try to stay away from cliffs or other places where there is no way out if things worsen. Look for caves and valleys for this purpose, but be sure that they aren't inhabited by animals, snakes, worms, or poisonous spiders. It would be wise to avoid sleeping in caves because you may wake up with a corpse next to you.

8) The more equipment that you have, the better. If you want to be ready for any disaster scenario, then it's best to be overprepared. Survival is all about being creative, so the only way to go is forward.

CALLING FOR HELP:
SIGNALS AND TOOLS

CHAPTER 12

SOS

SOS stands for the acronym Save Our Souls and has been used by various cultures across the world to symbolize reaching out for help in times of distress. It can refer to a person's bold decision to face severe consequences and be rescued, or it can refer to an act of solidarity with refugees fleeing their homeland.

Morse Code

Morse Code: The Alphabet of SOS

It was invented in May 1844 by Samuel Morse. The code allowed you to use letters and characters, The system, is used to send messages. It involved symbols: Is mean work is to use long beeps, short beeps, and paused to send the letters. Morse Code is commonly used in SOS because it is simple and easy to use with voice communications. The letters in Morse Code represent short and long transmissions (called dashes) that correspond to different signal strengths. The letters themselves were developed by Samuel Morse and his telegraph inventor, Alfred Vail.

The most famous of Morse Code's letters is Q, which is used to indicate that the message being sent is more than one dot long. The letter W stands for a long dash and the letter S for a short dash. Likewise, I (for "is" or "I am") and O (or "zero") stand for the start and end of transmissions; respectively; while N (for "not") can be used to cancel dots or dashes on a transmission.

Some of the more common letters are easier to translate than others. For example, A is ".-" or ".- -." while J is simply "--."

How to Translate SOS into Morse Code

So now that you know all about SOS and Morse Code, how do you convert an SOS signal into ones and zeros? Of course there are lots of sites on the internet that can help you do this digitally via an online converter, but if you want to learn the simple way on how to translate SOS into Morse Code without any fancy tools, follow these steps.

Step 1: Count the dashes. Three dashes followed by three long dashes make up an SOS distress signal. Each dash is longer than the one before, so this time you should count where the first short dash starts and where the last short dash ends.

Step 2: Count how many times a letter repeats. SOS is three letters long, which means that it isn't hard to work out how to translate SOS into Morse Code. You just need to note down how many times each letter appears.

SOS = .—.—.— = .- - -.- = .—.-.—

SOS stands for "Save Our Ship" or "Save Our Souls". The first part of the message is actually easy to translate since it's just three dots ("-") separated by two spaces ("-"). The next part is a little trickier, but you just need to count the times that each letter is written out. Thanks to Morse Code, you can use numbers to represent letters instead of having to memorize all 26 of them!

The first letter is "S" and it's three times long. That means that its Morse Code equivalent is a dash that's three times long. Likewise, the next letter is an "O" and it's once long. When Morse Code converts from letters to dots and dashes, a dash that's one time long becomes a dot. These two letters are represented by "-.-" in Morse Code, which means you can write out SOS as .-.-.

The last letter is a "K," and despite its appearance, it's not very long. It's only once long and can be shortened to "−" or written out as -.-.

Now that you know how to translate SOS into Morse Code, you can take all of this knowledge and use it to convert SOS into ones and zeros! The process for converting an SOS distress signal is straightforward, but there are a few different ways that you can go about it. The easiest way is to identify the letter that's used in SOS and then decode your message using the exact same letter in Morse Code (e.g., Q for "Q").

Variations of SOS Signals

There are many ways of saying "SOS" in the wilderness. Here are some you may have never heard of:

- Send out smoke signals by igniting natural material to produce thick, black smoke—a form of danger signal used by primitive tribes to warn neighboring villages or hunting parties. You can use anything from leaves, grasses, dry bark or pine needles to pitch. To make this signal you will need the following materials: 2 pieces of dry, clean bark or pine needles, 1 piece of dry wood for fire, half a roll of toilet paper.

The following method of preparing this signal is the most efficient. First prepare your fire by laying your dry wood on top of the coals of your campfire. Next, rub some toilet paper over both pieces of bark so that all kinks are removed. Light the paper with fire and cover it with coals. Let it burn for five minutes or so, after which take out the hot piece of burnt bark and get to work with your knife. Slash or chop at the bark until you have a hole large enough to fit your stick through. Slide the stick through the hole until the entire stick is through. Work your hand up and down the stick, rubbing off the ashes that are left behind. It is now ready for use.

- Shoot out soot by igniting natural material—a form of danger signal used by primitive tribes to warn neighboring villages or hunting parties. You can use anything from leaves, grasses, dry bark or pine needles to pitch. To make this signal you will need the following materials: 2 pieces of dry, clean bark or pine needles 1 piece of dry wood for fire half a roll of toilet paper The following method of preparing this signal is the most efficient First prepare your fire by laying your dry wood on top of the coals of your campfire. Get your toilet paper ready for use by ripping off the covering on one end. Next, you need to get the toilet paper lit. To achieve this purpose, build your fire up to a height of 1 foot and place the paper directly onto the fire. It should take four minutes or so for it to catch on fire, during which time you should gently blow on it. Once you have gotten it started, pour some water over your wood so that it will burn up more readily and add smoke together with black soot while at the same time emitting large amounts of heat and light. The signal should burn for about an hour. When you are satisfied that it is properly burning, hose off the fire and weed out the ashes of the fire pit.

- Scream Oh Shit by igniting natural material—a form of danger signal used by primitive tribes to warn neighboring villages or hunting parties. You can use anything from leaves, grasses, dry bark or pine needles to pitch. To make this signal you will need the following materials: 1 piece of dry wood for fire half a roll of toilet paper The following method of preparing this signal is the most efficient First prepare your fire by laying your dry wood on top of the coals of your campfire. Get your toilet paper ready for use by ripping off the covering on one end. Next, you need to get the toilet paper lit. To achieve this purpose, build your fire up to a height of 1 foot and place the paper directly onto the fire. It should take four minutes or so for it to catch on fire, during which time you should gently blow on it. Once you have gotten it started, pour some water over your wood so that it will burn up more readily and add smoke together with black soot while at the same time emitting large amounts of heat and light. The signal should burn for about an hour. When you are satisfied that it is properly burning, hose off the fire and weed out the ashes of the fire pit.

- Scrape Out Shit by igniting natural material—a form of danger signal used by primitive tribes to warn neighboring villages or hunting parties. You can use anything from leaves, grasses, dry bark or pine needles to pitch. To make this signal you will need the following materials: 1 piece of dry wood for fire half a roll of toilet paper The following method of preparing this signal is the most efficient First prepare your fire by laying your dry wood on top of the coals of your campfire. Get your toilet paper ready for use by ripping off the covering on one end. Next, you need to get the toilet paper lit. To achieve this purpose, build your fire up to a height of 1 foot and place the paper directly onto the fire. It should take four minutes or so for it to catch on fire, during which time you should gently blow on it. Once you have gotten it started, pour some water over your wood so that it will burn up more readily and add smoke together with black soot while at the same time emitting large amounts of heat and light. The signal should burn for about an hour. When you are satisfied that it is properly burning, hose off the fire and weed out the ashes of the fire pit.

- Shout Ouch! by igniting natural material—a form of danger signal used by primitive tribes to warn neighboring villages or hunting parties. You can use anything from leaves, grasses, dry bark or pine needles to pitch. To make this signal you will need the following materials: 1 piece of dry wood for fire half a roll of toilet paper The following method of preparing this signal is the most efficient First prepare your fire by laying your dry wood on top of the coals of your campfire. Get your toilet paper ready for use by ripping off the covering on one end. Next, you need to get the toilet paper lit. To achieve this purpose, build your fire up to a height of 1 foot and place the paper directly onto the fire. It should take four minutes or so for it to catch on fire, during which time you should gently blow on it. Once you have gotten it started, pour some water over your wood so that it will burn up more readily and add smoke together with black soot while at the same time emitting large amounts of heat and light. The signal should burn for about an hour. When you are satisfied that it is properly burning, hose off the fire and weed out the ashes of the fire pit.

CONCLUSION

As you reach the end of this book, I feel positively optimistic that you must have decoded the essential bushcraft skills to make a home in the wilderness for yourself. I have condensed my years of experience in the wilderness to present you an in-depth narrative of understanding the wilderness.

For many, being in the outdoors is a way of life, whether you enjoy hunting, fishing, backpacking, camping or just taking a hike.

Outdoor survival is about learning to achieve your goals in the wild through planning and preparation rather than purely relying on luck or chance through modern conveniences like GPS devices. It's about exploring natural areas without easy access to civilization where it might be necessary to improvise tools from equipment you already have on hand or forge your own items using traditional methods.

Outdoor Survival isn't the sole territory of decorated military personnel as they successfully take on and complete mission after mission in a wide range of territories and circumstances across the globe. It's a skillset and philosophy about being at home in nature that anyone can learn, appreciate, and employ. Even better yet, it's one of those skill sets that is invaluable as it could save your life if you ever found yourself having to rough it in the wilderness.

Surviving outdoor is a challenging and rewarding that can be enjoyed by anybody, regardless of age and fitness level. With the right tools, materials, and knowledge, you'll be able to enjoy outdoor life as much as those who have been doing it for years.

Accidents happen, people get lost, situations turn from idyllic to unpleasant or downright catastrophic in a matter of moments, and it can happen to anyone, at any time. Using bushcraft to tap into invaluable survival skills and knowledge of being at home in nature can prove to be your biggest ally in making the most of a situation that has gone awry.

Through this book we have equipped you with some of the best basic knowledge about wilderness skills from how to find your way around using the sun and night sky to lighting a fire and building a shelter that will protect you from the elements. We have included a wide range of other important information such as the basic bushcraft tools and supplies you should have. We've told you how to set basic snares and hunt when you have no experience or hunting tools. We have also provided basic first aid and other practical skills and knowledge, all of which come together to equip you to face adversity and rise above it.

According to popular belief, survivalists are doom and gloom types who warn about epidemics, natural calamities and nuclear war. According to their various experiences, this is far from reality. When calamity strikes, we don't merely throw up our hands and hope for the best. We take action to make things better.

Survival is not one of those things that people prepare for and practice often. It's easy to think that it will never happen to you. But it can, and when it does, the most important thing is your ability to use what you have around you to find a way out.

Printed in Great Britain
by Amazon

14217779R10086